"If I can keep even one kid
in school to get an education
and keep him away from drugs,
that's what I live for now."

—Ron Rearick

"A great story. A page turner. The kind I like to read and I wish I had written." JAMIE BUCKINGHAM

ICEMAN

A TRUE STORY

RON REARICK
WITH DOUG MURREN

Regal Books
A Division of GL Publications
Ventura, California, U.S.A.

Published by Regal Books
A Division of GL Publications
Ventura, California 93006
Printed in U.S.A.

Library of Congress Catalog in Publication Data

Rearick, Ron.
  Iceman.

  1. Rearick, Ron. 2. Crime and criminals—United States—
Biography. 3. Rehabilitation of criminals—United States.
4. Conversion. I. Murren, Doug
1951-   . II. Title.
HV6248.R393R42   1987   364.1′552′0924 [B]   86-33917
ISBN 0-8307-1124-4

1 2 3 4 5 6 7 8 9 10 / 91 90 89 88 87

Rights for publishing this book in other languages are contracted by Gospel
Literature International (GLINT) foundation. GLINT also provides technical
help for the adaptation, translation, and publishing of Bible study resources
and books in scores of languages worldwide. For further information, contact
GLINT, Post Office Box 488, Rosemead, California 91770, U.S.A., or the
publisher.

Dedicated
to
Billee Jean and Ron Murphy

Contents

Foreword

I believe Jesus had a special place in His heart for tough guys. He still does. I'm talking about the men of this world who never had it easy. Who had to overcome huge handicaps because no one would help them in their early years.

Ron was one of those tough guys. Was, and is. Unwanted at home, misunderstood at school, he had no choice but to make it on his own. He made it with his cunning mind and his strong arms. He took the only road open, the road of crime.

He was involved in it all: physical violence, theft, drug sales, the "mob," and eventually an airline hijack. His criminal friends dubbed him "Iceman" because his cold heart feared nothing and no one—not even the "hanging judge" who sentenced him to prison for 25 years.

Many lives end there, for today's prisons are filled with brilliant men and women who never had a chance. Society calls them "animals," "perverts" and "hardened criminals." They are tough guys. They have to be to survive.

But God does not look on the outer expression. He

looks on the heart. God saw something in Ron that no one else had seen. He saw a man with an unusual ability to help other men and women like him—other icemen and icewomen. So God went to work on the judge who had sentenced Ron, softening his heart. At the same time He went to work on Ron, melting the ice.

It's a great story. A page-turner. The kind I like to read—and wish I had written.

I'm grateful I had a small part in it. I read it while Doug Murren was writing it—and made a few suggestions. But I wasn't really reading it as an editor. I was reading it as an excited reader.

Who is Iceman? He's every kid who had to come up the hard way, who had to overcome huge handicaps, who felt no one ever cared, who knew God only as the Ultimate Cop. He is all of us with cold hearts.

This book is for prisoners—and for those who want to understand prisoners. Not just the men and women behind bars, but those caught in all the prisons of life: kids in bad homes, partners in bad marriages, workers in bad jobs, or no jobs, people with physical handicaps—for in every prison God is still at work, changing impossible circumstances, melting icy hearts and putting tough guys into ministry.

There's still hope. *Iceman* proves it.

Jamie Buckingham

Preface

What kind of person could possibly be called "Iceman"? The answer to that question, you'll discover, is a journey—a journey down a path that led to the most amazing of places and finally ended in the prison yard of McNeil Island Penitentiary.

Who is "Iceman"? He's Ron Rearick, a man who has spent 20 years of his life in prison. A man raised by an alcoholic father. A man declared by this world as incorrigible, an habitual criminal worthy only of incarceration in the toughest prisons available.

What did "Iceman" do? Probably more crimes than could be listed. He's known most notably for having hijacked a million dollars from United Airlines.

How did "Iceman" get freed from prison? It was nothing short of a miracle. You'll discover that in his exciting story.

Where's "Iceman" headed? The closing chapters of the book will tell us. The man once marked as an habitual criminal, a scourge and disease upon society, is in fact now one of the most thrilling speakers in high school assemblies and gatherings of all kinds of people across the United States.

Ron is a man whose life was miraculously transformed in a very simple way. A man committed now to making a serious dent in the drug culture. A man committed to, in his own words, "Keeping just one kid from going the way I did."

Join us in this exciting journey.

Acknowledgments

Any book the type of *Iceman* is always a team effort. As supportive author I would like to express thanks on the parts of both myself and Ron.

I must first extend a great deal of appreciation to our friend Jamie Buckingham. Jamie made valuable time available to give editorial advice that was incisive, corrective and irreplaceable.

I would also like to thank Earl Roe who convinced us to change the story to first person, which in turn allowed us to retain a lot of the dynamics and enthusiasm we were after.

Thanks to Mari Hanes, Ken Diehl and Pete Finch for their work on the earlier book they developed with Ron, also entitled *Iceman.* That became the skeleton to which we added the flesh of many additional living events.

In the preparation of the text, I would be remiss if I didn't thank Barb Shurin for typing and retyping the text. She saved us days in the presentation of the final draft. Her wise and careful scrutiny in watching for inconsistencies in the story line was also invaluable.

I also have to thank the dozens of high school principals who allowed me to come along with Ron as I took notes and made observations in the halls and in private interviews with Ron and students over many long months. Without this it would have been impossible to catch a sense of the power of Ron's stories as presented to groups of hundreds of high school students.

Finally, I'd like to thank Vivian Brodine, my secretary, and the congregation at Eastside Foursquare Church for their understanding when Ron and I would slip away for several days to polish up the text.

And thanks to everyone who prayed for the book in the process of its development.

1

The Plaque—Not the Plane!

American Airlines Flight No. 673, from Harrisburg, Pennsylvania to Chicago, was an inaugural flight. The plane was set to fly July 2, 1984. Dignitaries ranging from the president of American Airlines to the mayors from the surrounding cities were at the airport to celebrate.

Hors d'oeuvres were being served under a large, yellow canopy on the taxiway. Everyone was sipping champagne. From all appearances, it seemed to be a normal promotional affair. Finally, it was time for an airline official to present a plaque along with a first-class ticket to the first passenger. Then everything came unglued.

The young woman took the plaque from the table near the podium and handed it to the slightly graying, 40-year-old man who stood grinning at the base of the steps leading up to the DC-9. News cameras flashed and TV cameras rolled. As the man accepted the bronzed plaque, he, in return, handed the woman airline official a thin, blue book. She glanced down. The cover featured the picture of a man's face inside a block of melting ice. The word *Iceman* in bold, white letters was blazoned across the top of the book.

She thanked him and started to turn away. But something caught her eye. Glancing down, she noticed the copy on the back of the book: "In 1972, Iceman extorted one million dollars from United Airlines! He was sentenced to 25 years at McNeil Island Federal Prison."

Iceman! Everyone in the airline industry was familiar with that name and that infamous case. An armed hijacker, known as Iceman, had threatened to blow up a United Airline's plane loaded with passengers and being readied for takeoff, and he came within a hair of escaping with a $1-million ransom!

Instead, he'd been captured, tried and sentenced to prison. Everyone figured he would be there for life. Now, here he was, brashly boarding an American Airlines flight!

She gasped audibly and whirled around to the group of officials behind her. There was a quick huddle. Sensing something was wrong, the politicians discreetly stepped away from where the TV cameras were focused. The airline officials were talking excitedly. They stared at the book; they looked over at Ron; they looked back at the book. Yes, it was the same man—Ron Rearick, who, 12 years before, had extorted $1 million from United Airlines, using the ruse of a bomb threat. How had he gotten out of prison? they asked each other. What was he doing here? Was this a joke or a threat?

They glanced back again at Ron, who was standing quietly in the sun, smiling. Of course, they didn't know what had transpired in his life since 1972. How could they know that he had just come from a high school in Harrisburg, where he had spent the morning telling his incredible life story to several hundred fascinated students. All they knew was that a former hijacker was now boarding *their* plane—and the cameras were rolling.

It was not a threat. Nor was it a joke. Instead, events had simply converged to allow the most dangerous hijacker in America—now an evangelist for Jesus Christ—to be first in line to board the airline's inaugural flight to Chicago.

"Take the plaque—not the plane," Paul Harvey, the news commentator, joked the next day on his nationwide radio program. He related the unusual story, and how the airline officials were finally convinced that Ron Rearick was now a changed man, that he had no intention of hijacking their plane, and how they allowed him to board the plane at the Harrisburg Airport.

But what happened 12 years earlier was no joke. Settling down in his seat, Ron chuckled at the coincidence. Since God had taken control of his life every day was like this, it seemed.

"God, you really do have a sense of humor," he grinned.

Then Ron let his memory drift back over the years. Suddenly, it was July 1972 and he had just pulled off the sweltering Utah highway to wait for the $1 million to be dropped.

2

Planning the Heist

The drop point was on a lonely, deserted stretch of two-lane road, a few miles south of Salt Lake City. I pulled the car off the road, facing the oncoming traffic. My partner Stubs's directions to the airline officials had been specific: "Drop the money off by the bridge, or the next flight will be blown up on the runway."

Now it was time to wait. I watched as each car passed. Heat waves curled up from the pavement in front and behind me. My vision through the rearview mirror was distorted. I could hear myself breathing. It seemed to get louder all the time. My heart was pounding wildly and drops of sweat poured off my head. Every nerve had heightened to supersensory levels.

"Where is that Chevy with the million?" I mumbled. I gripped the steering wheel harder, and each time a car passed, my teeth pressed deeper into my lower lip.

Even though I was called Iceman, I'd never pulled off a job this big before. I'd never even seen a million bucks before. But that's what I was waiting for: one cool million!

My partner Stubs and I had made the calls to United Airlines. Our plan had been laid out well for the getaway. This final heist would, at last, end my bondage to The Mob and fix me up for some real livin': some nice condos, two or three chicks and plenty of money to do just about anything I wanted to.

Being a strong arm for The Mob was like being their slave. Being "owned" by someone else was no way to live. I'd been their "collection man" for a long time. But I'd had enough of it. This plan was my way out. The money would set me free from all this arm breaking and "muscling" for Vic and "The Family." No more fear of prison, a million bucks, freedom and happiness at last.

I glanced up one more time in the rearview mirror, the whole time keeping a good eye on the road ahead. As I squinted, I could see how crooked my nose was. I couldn't remember how many times my nose had been broken, but it really was a sight! It seemed to go four ways at once. I grinned. *I won't have to worry about duckin' anymore because my fightin' days are over. Rich men don't do their own fighting. They pay someone else to do it.*

"Keep cool, Man!" I muttered. "It's gonna come off, Man. It's gonna come off."

It didn't take long to cover the floorboard of my car with cigarette butts. I was smoking one after another.

A car with a shield painted on its door passed by. I scrunched down in the seat. "Damn! It's a county health inspector!" My mouth totally went dry. This was too well planned to fail. Once again, I went over the plan—every detail—as I wiped my forehead with my forearm. My mind returned to the day we'd planned this caper. I knew it couldn't fail.

I'd been sitting alone at the bar in the Stardust Hotel in

Las Vegas. I had a half-empty whiskey glass in front of me as I brooded over a drug delivery that had turned sour. It was a bad deal. Some kid, probably working out of the local high school off the Vegas Strip, came by to pick up his dope. The fool kid didn't have the money. I'd always made it very clear that it was cash up front, 'cuz you couldn't trust those druggies.

I started to rough the kid up a little to remind him who the boss of this operation was. After all, I couldn't have any of these kids taking advantage of me. Word would get out, and first thing you know, Rearick, instead of Iceman, would be known as a pushover. First thing you know, you're in over your head with your own dope bills.

The idiot kid pulled a .22 pistol on me! I was caught totally off guard. What was a kid doin' with a weapon like this, I wondered. Moving like a cat, I grabbed the pistol and used the butt of the gun to teach the punk a lesson. I left him bleeding in the alley. I was really hoping no one would find him; the punk deserved to lie there in agony. After all, he'd messed with Iceman.

Maybe it was the gun that unnerved me that day. I didn't mind using muscle, but I'd always hated weapons. I'd seen more than one guy taken out by some crazy punk druggie, who didn't know what he was doing, and panicked. I always figured that the last thing I needed was getting trigger-happy myself and end up shooting some kid. Then I'd have the whole country on my back. I really had to use a weapon seriously only once, in Mexico. I didn't plan on having to use one in the States. I knew, with my record, I'd get chased down and caught, and that would be it for old Rearick.

"God! When will all this end?" I remember muttering as I knocked the glass over on the counter and two or three guys looked over at me. I knew what I needed: money—and lots of it! That's all I needed. If I just had enough money, it would put an end to all this craziness.

And that's when the plan was birthed. It was like a eureka moment. The discovery of gold and the flash of a plan came to me, just like that. I knew all I needed was a new idea. I'd always been good at that. At crucial moments, Vic and the guys depended on me for a new escape route or some way to improve the drug racket. Most of my buddies were in prison or dead because they stayed in the same scene too long. I knew I had to be different. I couldn't stand prison anymore. But then, maybe, it would be better if I were dead, I thought, as I ordered another drink.

Earlier in the evening, I'd watched the news on the TV in the bar. There were stories of several hijackings that had happened since March of that year.

All at once, the idea came to me. The terrorist groups were using airline hijackings to get publicity for their causes. It just might work for me, too. Maybe hijacking was a simpler way to get money than I thought. I chuckled and mused over it as I stirred my drink with the swizzle stick, poking at the chunks of ice.

Most of the hijackers failed because they were political fanatics and not careful enough planners, I reasoned. Me? I had connections to score really big. With the right weapons and my knowledge of explosives, it'd be a snap! It'd be like stealing candy from a baby. I began to draw out the plan on a napkin.

When I got back to Salt Lake City, I found that my old buddy Stubs Reilly was in town. Stubs had shown up in Salt Lake after a stint in Soledad Prison. I was sure it was fate. Now, here was a guy with real nerve. Stubs and I went way back. We met in the Army and, together, we'd pulled off some pretty slick moves and some fantastic parties.

Stubs looked just like his name: squatty, with stubby arms and legs and a tree trunk for a torso. Even his hair was stubby-looking. He'd kept it in a crew cut since his Army days, even though it was now way out-of-date.

By the time the third game of pool was played, we had our plan. I figured that the mistake other hijackers had made was that they tried to take a plane while it was in the air. I'd heard about D.B. Cooper. One thing I had to say for Cooper: He sure had nerve. But I sure didn't want to parachute from a plane at the time of year he did! No sir. B-r-r. They never did find the guy either. It wasn't the kind of storybook ending I had envisioned for myself.

So I decided it would be a lot easier to blow up a plane while it was still on the ground. I knew better than to risk having a passenger take explosives on board, so I arranged to have a bomb loaded with the luggage. It just so happened that one of the cargo loaders for United Airlines owed me a big favor. We readied the explosives.

Stubs and I had a map of the Salt Lake airport. We studied it, restudied it, and studied it some more. We checked out all the roads around Salt Lake City and, together, scrutinized a number of drop-off points.

Then it came time to head back East and pick up the "fire power." We figured we'd have to deal not only with the local cops, but with a whole army of Feds as well—maybe a lot more.

In dealing with the Feds, the first thing we had to do was use our heads. So we devised a plan. We'd have the airlines' guy delivering the money go from one phone booth to another while we observed how many FBI men were trailing him. Then we'd simply lie in wait and blow them all off the road.

We decided to use a Browning automatic rifle (BAR) as our main weapon. Stubs brought back a beauty from his first trip to the East Coast. A BAR could cut a *bus* in two! We belly laughed as we anticipated seeing the car loaded with Feds being blown off the road.

We practiced using the BAR. After we blew in half several large, wooden targets, we figured we were ready for the hijacking. Stubs bought some armor-piercing bullets— just to make sure the job would be done right.

The target date arrived two weeks later. However, a rash of hijackings caused security at the airports to tighten and we had to change our plans radically. I was furious!

Stubs buried his face in his hands as he read the bold print on the front page of Salt Lake's newspaper: "Security Tightened at All U.S. Airports."

Suddenly, I brightened as an inspiration came to me.

"Hey, Stubs, we're not outta the game yet. This could make our job a lot easier. In fact, maybe we don't even have to get a bomb on the plane. There's no chance that our contact at the airlines is goin' to get the bomb through now. Maybe it just saves us havin' another guy who could turn us in involved.

"Hey, Man, we've got it made! The airlines are all set up for us. Those dudes are runnin' scared as rabbits with all the crazy hijackers. We don't hafta risk puttin' a bomb on the plane. We'll just tell 'em on the phone that we've planted a bomb on the plane, even though we really haven't. They'll believe us and we won't give 'em time to find out any different!"

3

The Big Day

I stuck my head out the window to make sure I had a clear view. *Nope, no cars coming down the road.* I leaned back, blew my nose, wiped my forehead with my arm and muttered, "I wish they'd hurry up."

It was Stubs who had made the phone calls. Our plan called for a series of calls to be made from different phone booths so they'd be hard to trace. I stood listening as Stubs whispered huskily through two handkerchiefs. The first time, he spoke only a few sentences.

"Mr. Jones, there's a remote-controlled bomb on Flight 606, which you just loaded at Gate 11. Call 'em and tell 'em to freeze. No one gets off that plane and no one else gets on, ya understand? Just keep cool, Mr. Jones, and sit there in your nice, big leather chair until you hear from me again."

"Stubs, do you think he bought the bluff? Maybe we shoulda used our baggage handler, after all."

"Naw, Man. He was so shook, I bet he wet his pants."

Ten minutes later, Stubs made the second call from a different phone.

"Mr. Jones, in exactly one hour we want $1 million, in

unmarked hundred-dollar bills. Just leave the plane and people on the runway. If anyone goes to check the plane—blast-off! Understand? We won't negotiate. This is the only time we're goin' to ask. You're the delivery boy, Jones. Don't send anyone else, or you and your passengers are dead ducks. Get the million, put it in a flight bag and go to the phone booth at Twenty-First and Temple. If anyone's with ya, the plane goes ka-boom anyway! Understand?"

We figured there was bound to be a tail. Jones, of course, had called the FBI the minute Stubs hung up. But we were prepared. Our plan was perfect. I had parked in a supermarket parking lot, adjacent to the phone booth. One hour later, a white Cadillac pulled up to the curb. A well-dressed, but very nervous, man got out, carrying a blue and white flight bag.

The moment Jones reached the phone booth, the phone rang. Nervously, Jones answered, glancing up and down the street.

"Jones, leave your car where it is. If the Feds on the back floor of your car follow you, they're dead men too! Get in the green Chevy parked at the corner. There's a key in the ignition. Drive to the phone booth at the corner of Redwood Road and Thirteenth Street South. Wait for another call."

I watched the green Chevy pull away. No cars followed. Within seconds, I passed the Chevy and was waiting across the street when Jones pulled up. I flicked the switch on the walkie-talkie. "He's here, Stubs."

When Jones reached the second booth, the phone rang. Again, I watched from a distance. It was Stubs, all right. I could tell by the look on Jones's face. Stubs directed him to a third phone booth.

25

This time, I noticed something else, a brown sedan. It was the same one I saw at the first booth. Yep, there was only one car trailing Jones, and I could see three men. Maybe more were hiding on the floor of the backseat.

It was time for me to head out to the final outpost at Jordan River Gulch. I called Stubs on the CB radio.

"Hey, good Buddy, I'm back from my huntin' trip and I only saw one mule deer."

Stubs then directed Jones to go to the Jordan River overpass. He was told to fling the flight bag over the right side of the bridge without even stopping his car—"just toss it out the window." Stubs made his last call from a gas station, about two miles from the uninhabited area around the Jordan River Gulch. There'd been plenty of time to get the BAR set up. The rest was up to us.

The plan called for me to run over, grab the money, then race to a nearby plateau where a twin-engine Cessna was waiting. I was to start the engines while I waited for Stubs, who would pilot the plane.

I found myself saying, over and over again, under my breath: "Keep calm, Man. Keep cool. It's gonna work. It's workin' just fine. It's got to work! You know the car with the money is comin'."

I could see the sunlight reflecting off a car in the distance as it came into view. My heart pounded wildly, then seemed to stand still a moment before it beat hard again as I nervously waited.

I watched until I was certain it was the green Chevy. I could see up the hill for a distance and spotted the blue and white flight bag as it was being hurled over the bridge to the gulch below. The green car sped away.

It was awesomely quiet as I waited a few moments. What had happened to the brown sedan? I wondered.

Maybe it wasn't the Feds in that car, after all. Maybe it was just my imagination. That sure would make it a lot easier.

It was time to go. I started the car, drove down the incline and back onto the road. I knew I had to move like lightning. If the cops were there, I'd hear them. But there was only silence.

I jumped out of the car, leaving the door open to save time after I retrieved the bag. I slid down the sandy bank of the creek bed. With a loud Indian whoop, I shouted: "There it is! Our million dollars!" I couldn't believe our luck. There hadn't been any double-cross.

I looked inside and saw all the crisp hundred-dollar bills. I paused . . . listening. No sounds. I decided to count it all—right there. Stuffing the last bills back in the bag, I was suddenly seized with panic. How long had I taken? How much precious time had I lost? Then I was gripped by another thought. "Why didn't we ask for more? Oh, God!" My curse echoed through the desert. "It's not enough! It's not going to be enough! I know, Man, it's not going to be enough!"

I began yelling, almost uncontrollably, as I ran back to the car. I jumped in, slammed the door and quickly headed toward the small plane field on the plateau where the Cessna was waiting for our getaway.

Fifty yards down the road, I rolled down the window so I could hear the BAR knock the Feds off the road. But I heard nothing. Strange. I pulled over and waited. I listened and listened some more. Then I stuck my head out the window so I could hear better. Silence. There was no explosive gunfire telling me that Stubs and the BAR were blowing the Feds off the road.

"Come on, Stubs! Let 'em have it! Come on, Man!"

But there was no gunfire. I began screaming. "Damn it, Stubs, shoot 'em! I'm not leavin' 'till I hear you blow 'em away!"

I could see cars approaching fast. Then, suddenly, the dusk was ignited with explosive light! The blast of light startled me, magnified because it had come on me so suddenly. I instinctively knew the headlights were from the Feds' car and that the searchlights were coming from vans that followed close behind.

I wheeled my Camaro back onto the road and floorboarded the thing. Tires squealed; dust flew.

If I can just get ahead of them a bit, I can make it to the cutoff to the plane. Maybe I can figure out how to fly that thing, even without Stubs. Maybe Stubs has gone on ahead to the plane.

I bounded up over a small hill on the road. Suddenly, I realized I was headed right smack into a roadblock. Three patrol cars were there waiting. I slammed on the brakes and braced myself, as my tires screeched across the cement and laid down a black trail of burning rubber. As the car came to a sliding, screeching halt, sand and gravel spewed onto the police cars.

Where's my gun? The seat was empty. Had it fallen out? I figured I'd be a dead man anyway if I tried to shoot it out. So I just slumped over the wheel and raised my hands in surrender. There were enough Feds, plain clothesmen and uniformed cops to take Vietnam! It's a good thing I couldn't find my gun and try to shoot it out, because there were enough guns pointed at me to turn me into a sieve.

I began berating myself, "You fool! If you hadn't waited to count the money or pulled over to listen for the gun, you'd been at the plane by now! You idiot! Man, where's Stubs?"

The Feds came over, yanked me out of the seat, threw me over the hood of the car and frisked me.

I yelped, "Hey, come on, Man, take it easy! I haven't done anything! I'm tryin' to help you guys out!"

My mind began racing for an alibi, for some explanation to get me out of this mess.

"Hey, Guys, I haven't done anything! What's goin' on? What're you guys after, anyway?"

A typical, FBI-lookin' kind of a guy grabbed my shoulders, spun me around and growled, "If you're up to nothin', then what're you doin' out here? Why did you take off so fast? And what's this bundle of money?"

My mind finally engaged. "I was just headed into Salt Lake when the oil light in my car came on. So I pulled over to the side of the road to look at it. Next thing I know, this guy threw somethin' out his window. He was goin' so fast, I didn't even see what the car looked like. So I waited a few minutes. I was goin' to pick it up and turn it into the cops, 'cuz I figured some guy'd lost his baggage. Then I opened it up and, lordy, I found that airline bag stuffed with money. There must be thousands there. Let me tell ya, I was afraid. I figured it had been stolen, so I was just on my way to the sheriff's now to turn it in. Then you guys come from outta nowhere and act like you're goin' to blow my head off!"

The lieutenant barked, "Let's take him in! Read him his rights!" Instantly, my hands were yanked behind my back and I felt the cuffs clank on my wrists.

"Why didja start runnin', Flake?"

"I don't know. I didn't know you guys were the police. I saw those lights. I didn't hear any sirens. You scared the daylights outta me. For all I knew, you were after the guy who tossed the money over the bridge."

29

In the meantime, the plain clothesmen were tearing my car apart. One of them shouted, "Lieutenant Nielson, we can't find a weapon of any kind."

The cop's eyebrows shot up and he registered surprise. I tried to look nonchalant, though I was sure I had a .38 sitting on the front seat. *The gun couldn't have just disappeared. What in the world happened to it?*

"Stay cool, Man," I kept reminding myself. "You're Iceman. You can bluff 'em if you stay cool."

Sitting in the backseat, the cuffs cutting into my wrists, I repeated to myself the alibi I'd just told the cop. I knew I'd have to stay consistent. I knew they'd be asking me over and over again about it. I'd been through this many times before. *Oh, God, don't let 'em check my record!*

"Let's take him to the courthouse before we question him any more," barked the head guy. "And leave a couple of cars here at the creek bed too. Jones and Friedman, you stay here and keep an eye out. If you see anything, call me and I'll be back out."

The ride to town didn't take long, but long enough for me to get burned up at Stubs, and gripped by fear. Then I calmed down. *Heck, these guys've got nothin' on me! My story makes sense. After all, this guy here is buyin' it.*

As we entered the courthouse, an FBI officer read me my rights again. They questioned me for about a half hour, and I answered everything real smooth and easy like. After all, I figured I didn't have anything to fear. First, the county sheriff asked me a bunch of questions, then an FBI man took his shot at me and, finally, an FAA man threw some more questions at me.

It was beginning to look a little comical to me. I mean, I felt I had successfully convinced all these guys that I was just a good ole boy who'd just love to be their buddy.

One of the cops came over and sat down beside me. He handed me a cigarette and a cup of coffee. "You might be in for a big reward," he said.

I grinned, "Well, I deserve it after all you guys have put me through."

I noticed the computer was chattering in the background. Several officers stood in front of the Teletype, reading as the paper spit from the machine. I moaned inwardly. Things had changed.

One of the men came over and abruptly took the cigarette out of my mouth, the coffee away and marched me out to the fingerprinting room.

"The joke's over, Rearick. We've got your record, and we're going to get the rest of your buddies involved in this thing too. Book him! No bail. Give him his call to his attorney and keep two men on him!"

The three cops marched me off and locked me up in a cell, all by myself.

Stubs had disappeared, never to be heard from again. But I had bigger worries than that. The penalty for attempted hijacking could be as high as 25 years in prison.

4

The Freeze Begins

My entire childhood, it seemed, had been spent moving from one school to another. All the mining towns were the same. None of them were too impressive, most of them really frightening to a little boy like me. The buildings always seemed to have that same gray gloom about them.

The schools were no different. They all had big entrances with kids standing around. They all had those big, heavy doors with the panic bars on the inside that were always loose for some reason. The paint was usually chipped off the bottom of the doors on both sides from kids kicking them. The windows were always smudged with grungy fingerprints.

Main Street in every mining town had a tavern I'd have to pass by. It always seemed like everyone was having so much fun in it. Then there'd be one of those funny little buildings that Pop called "cat houses."

Of course, there was always a small department store that sold all kinds of things. Often it was just a modified grocery store with everything from Levi jeans to apples.

All the elementary schools were gray and dirty-looking. The small playgrounds beside them were usually filled with potholes and the ground was packed hard as cement. No one in these towns seemed to care much if the kids had a soft field to play on.

Though all the mining towns had the same familiarity about them, there were still all those new faces on all those kids that seemed like an impossible challenge to me. Even at the age of nine, I'd hear people talk about the "edginess" of my eyes, the kind of eyes you often see in a wounded child. They'd dart back and forth quickly, trying to pick up on the moods and responses of the adult figures or my peers. They were the kind of eyes that showed a lot of sensitivity and reacted strongly to what others thought about me—quick to pick up every little hint of approval or disapproval. I could modify my behavior accordingly. I was a wounded child.

My family seemed to move about once a year. Pop would quit his job and head off to a new mine, hoping for more money or a better position. The one in Wrightwood was a lime mine. Pop had always worked silver and copper mines in the past, so this was a new venture for him.

Even if I wasn't excited about it, I was happy that Pop seemed pretty enthused. I had the secret hope that, maybe, if Pop found a job he liked, he'd quit drinking. I had tried so hard to be the kind of little boy my Pop'd like to be around at home instead of out drinking. But it never seemed to work that way.

Pop had had his hopes raised many times. Once, a small gold claim had stirred Pop's hopes higher than I'd ever seen them. The whole family was hopeful.

But, as usual, the moves from mining town to mining

town seemed to cause more trouble. Eventually, there'd be more drunkenness, more disappointment. Then off we'd go to another town.

My sister Violet was 15 years older than I. Sometimes I asked her how she managed all the moves from one town to another. Even my other sister Sue, who was five years younger than me, seemed to handle all the moves so well. I figured, maybe girls didn't mind moving as much as guys did. After all, girls can hide their fears with some sort of feminine mystique.

Reminiscing about my early days and the frequent moves always brought back the sad memory of my little brother Donny. "I wish Donny had lived," I'd say to myself. "Then I'd have another boy to play with, and there'd be someone else to understand how I feel."

Poor Donny died of pneumonia on a cold California night in one of the mining towns. Mom cried whenever Donny's name came up, and I'd hear her whispering, "He was such an angel. He would have been such a smart boy. He was such a good boy."

However, Mom never took the time to tell her other kids that she felt the same way about them. Of course, some mothers don't think of that. But in my child's mind, it seemed that the things that weren't said spoke volumes. All I knew, even at nine, was that I didn't feel like a "good" boy, and I knew, for sure, that I wasn't all that smart.

So, of course, I reasoned that Mom cried because Donny would have been everything I wasn't. At times, even though I couldn't understand my feelings, I felt as though *I* was somehow responsible for Donny's death. Down deep, I really knew that Momma didn't mean to make me feel that way, but I figured it was so, just the same.

Pop never knew how—nor even tried—to tell anybody he loved them, especially me, his son. At times I ached inside just to hear the words: "I love you, Son."

It seemed when I tried to get expressions of affection from Pop, he'd always push me away. Though I really knew, deep down, that Pop loved me, I didn't think Pop liked me. And to me—a little boy of nine—there was nothing more important in the whole world than to have my daddy like me.

Those early, post-World War II, baby-boom days brought crowded classrooms. The harried teachers had no time to spot a struggling boy like me. They were just trying to survive in their overcrowded classrooms. From the first day of school, I figured I was just one of the "dumb" kids anyway. When I got to the end of each school year, the teacher would pass me to the next grade just to get rid of me because I'd been such a discipline problem and she didn't want to cope with me anymore.

By the time I finished the first grade, the second-grade teacher had already heard about my reputation and planned to pass me on quickly to the third grade. All this happened without my ever developing reading skills. It seemed no one ever thought this would eventually catch up with me.

Though I had a little easier time with math, I had missed so many chunks of information in my earlier years that my basic development in reasoning and deduction had been impaired as well.

By the time I reached the fourth grade, I could barely read at all. The textbook words looked like mumbo jumbo. I spent most of my time staring out the windows or plotting some new scheme to attract the glancing, flirting eyes of one of the little girls in class.

Wrightwood Elementary was the grade school's name in Wrightwood, California. As usual, the first three days went smoothly enough. There were some nice kids in class, but right off I didn't see anyone I could relate to. I kept looking, though. I really wanted to be liked by the other kids and I needed approval more than anything else in the world.

The fatal day finally came when my geography teacher asked me a question. I didn't have the remotest idea what the answer was. My mouth felt as dry as a cottonball; my tongue felt like it weighed about 20 pounds. I stammered . . . paused . . . stuttered . . . paused again. Everyone began to laugh. Maybe they didn't laugh out loud, but I could tell by their grins that they were quite delighted that this new kid couldn't answer even a simple question. I could read in their eyes what they were thinking: Yep, this kid's a dummy all right.

I had one device that worked for me many times before. Though I didn't realize it, it was becoming a life-long pattern: Remove the attention from myself and focus it back on the teacher.

The furtive, quick-darting look in my eyes changed rapidly to a scowl and a defiant, penetrating glare, accompanied by a string of cuss words! Mrs. Comby was not ready for this. She was stunned. Her face turned bright red; her eyebrows shot up; she gasped, then screeched, "Ronny Rearick, get your body down to the principal's office this instant!"

My plan had worked well. I was now out of the center of attention; I got out of answering the question; and, once again, I'd definitely established myself as at least an interesting kid. Maybe now I'd even be popular. After all, nobody liked that teacher. Again, I'd hidden the fact that I was a dummy. For all they knew, I just had guts. I'd take a beating from the principal any day, anytime, rather than face the laughter and teasing of the other kids.

The next day, all proved well. My plan had worked again in this rough mining town. Most kids in mining towns respected a rough kid with guts, as most of the homes were like mine: torn and shattered by alcoholism, and constantly moving. All the kids seemed to recognize that my response to the teacher was a statement of authority—the kind of authority that only grade school kids know, that defiance to a teacher establishes courage.

As yet, however, I still didn't have a friend. I did notice, though, during several recess breaks, that two brothers, Frank and Sam, were the playground bullies. They always seemed to pick on a smaller kid, the same one they cornered nearly every day. I was growing to like the kid.

One day, I decided to let the bullies know I was nobody to mess with, especially with some kid *I* liked. The kid they'd chosen to pick on made it obvious to me they were not only a couple of chickens at heart, but bullies to boot.

Sure enough, the next noon hour Sam and Frank tripped the smaller boy and started needling him. But they went too far this time; they pushed the smaller kid's face into a mud puddle in the center of the playground.

I exploded inside! I couldn't stand to see bullies pick on little guys, as I always had a soft spot for losers—especially when they were put down by the "winners."

I raced over, grabbed a hunk of Frank's shirt and knocked him down. Then I knocked the wind out of him by jamming my foot in his stomach with all the force I could muster. Turning to Sam, who was stunned by my sudden attack, I slammed my fist into his surprised face! Sam's nose got real red, and blood began to trickle down to the corners of his mouth. Next, I quickly punched both of his eyes—pow! pow!—like a prize fighter. They immediately bruised and swelled up.

Out of nowhere, the teacher grabbed Sam, Frank and me. The outcome: All of us were expelled and told we could return to school only if we brought our folks with us.

Sam and Frank had it real easy. Their dad owned the local grocery store, which was a prestigious position in any mining town, so their fate didn't seem to linger with them as long as mine did with me. I was promptly labeled a problem.

But as far as the other kids were concerned, I was a "darned good fighter" and a "likable guy," because I'd beaten up the two most-disliked bullies in the school. As far as I was concerned, the only thing that mattered was what my peers thought of me. I was pretty proud of myself for taking on two older guys who outweighed me.

The next noon hour I was invited to join in a game of Red Rover. Now the other boys seemed to like hanging around me. My new strategy in life was to be rewarded. I'd gotten it down. This was how to get acceptance. I also discovered that once you're accepted, others become afraid of you and you don't have to fight anymore. It sure made life easier.

I didn't know at that time, however, that this strategy would lead me down more dismal paths in life than most men could travel in five lifetimes. My young mind did understand one thing, though: I was now liked!

Like many parents, mine tried to compensate for their inability to show affection by fostering an overly controlled environment. I experienced very little freedom to venture out into life on my own, so I really enjoyed it whenever I was freed from the influence of either of my folks, who always seemed to be breathing down my neck.

The results were tragic. Not only did I push to take advantage of any moment of freedom I could grasp, but I'd push even harder to see how far I could go.

At school things went peaceably enough for several months because Mrs. Comby didn't call on me. Of course, when question-and-answer time came, I usually managed to escape by ducking my head so she couldn't see me. One day, however, the inevitable happened. Mrs. Comby mustered her courage and singled Ron out once again.

"Ron, what is five times five?"

I was sure it was 25, but then again, maybe it wasn't. Five times five . . . h-m-m, let's see . . . five times five. I wanted to make sure it was 25; I didn't want anyone laughing at me. So I decided to stall matters by reaching down to tie my shoe. When I did, I found that a rock had slipped inside my shoe during recess.

The problem was that, as I stalled, Mrs. Comby interpreted it as defiance. Of course, almost constantly by now, I'd developed a look of defiance, so there was really no reason for the teacher to think otherwise.

The pitch in her voice rose a notch. "Ron, don't you dare take your shoes off in this class!"

"I've got a rock in there, Teacher, and I can't think while it's hurtin'!"

"Young man, if you take that shoe off in this class, you might as well get up and head out the door, and use those shoes to keep right on walking!"

I could handle this skirmish with the teacher, but I couldn't handle what I saw out of the corner of my eye: Two little girls—one with pink ribbons around her pigtails—were bobbing up and down, trying to stop laughing, each snickering with her hand clasped over her mouth.

Subconsciously, I thought, "This teacher's undoing all the respect it's taken me weeks to earn. That does it!"

Reaching down, I grabbed my math book and, without another thought, hurled it violently at the elderly Mrs. Comby, who was standing with her hands on her hips only about six feet away! The book slammed into her midsection like a cannonball! Flushed with rage, she doubled over in pain and sank to her knees. Suddenly, the room was ominously silent; no one moved.

Both frightened and angry, I started to run. In my frantic effort to beat a hasty retreat, I knocked Mrs. Comby down again—this time, accidentally—as she was struggling to her feet. I knew it was the end for me now.

Once outside, I could hear Mrs. Comby screaming. "You'll never get back into this school, Ron Rearick! Did you hear me? Never! Never!"

I'd blown it. I knew the answer was 25. Why didn't I just say 25? Why didn't I just give the answer? Why couldn't I be smart like Donny was? Why couldn't I be a good boy like he was? My right hand—the one that threw the book—kept shaking. I was numb with embarrassment and shame.

But that didn't matter now. Nothing mattered. Dad would beat me now, for sure, just short of death. And Mom would cry. I was just no good. But instead of feeling remorse, I figured it was a time to be hard—as hard as the playground I was running across toward home.

"Nobody'd better try to put me down again!" I repeated over and over, all the way home. "If they do, they'll be sorry. I'll fix 'em, just like I did Mrs. Comby!"

My heart was already freezing over—like ice.

5

The Early Days

Colton, California, in the 1950s, was one of the most troubled suburbs in Southern California. It was in this melting pot of violence that I began to discover myself.

Mostly, the town was comprised of Blacks and Chicanos, which was sometimes an embarrassment to me. You had to be a tough white guy to hold your own in that neck of the woods.

My folks seemed to be unaware of the impact that adolescence and a hostile environment had on me as I developed my own identity, an identity that sealed the course of my life for many years to come. Violence became my god, and pleasure my rewards.

In 1953 I entered junior high school. This time Pop had decided to move on ahead and try his hand at welding. Colton, being so close to Los Angeles, was an entirely different world than the small mining towns I'd grown up in. I quickly got into the "in" things of the day, and really loved the city life: peg pants, white T-shirts with high necks, black leather jackets, the whole bit. I was good at getting my DA (duck-style) haircut just right, and I imitated James

Dean's saunter perfectly. He was the movie idol of the mid-50s for us teens. Girls were known as *tweaks*.

Now the kids around San Bernardino knew Colton to be a war zone. Almost like franchises, the streets were divided into sections among the various groups. Rumbles were intense and constant occurrences. The Whites liked to pit themselves against the Blacks, the Blacks would gang up on the Orientals and the Chicanos would take on anybody. Most of the time, though, it was everyone against everyone else. But if the truth were known, everybody was really scared to death the whole time.

On my second day of school in Colton Junior High, I got confused and ended up in the wrong homeroom. When my name wasn't called from the roll, I raised my hand and asked why.

"Because you're not supposed to be here. This isn't your homeroom," the teacher replied.

The boy across the aisle from me made some smart-aleck remark. It was all I needed to explode. With one strong swing I knocked the boy clear out of his chair. The principal appeared and I was expelled for three days. The rest of the year was worse. That was also the year I started making pitches for the tweaks.

The day was real special when I was able to attract the attention of a dimple-faced blond girl named Marilyn. She was a real catch, all right. A tall ninth-grader had walked by and slapped her on the bottom. Embarrassed, she turned around just in time to see me deck the guy. Immediately, I became her knight in shining armor.

There was just one problem: The ninth-grader turned out to be the leader of one of the school's strongest gangs. That night was challenge time when the kid threatened to kill me while his gang looked on.

"Hey, Man, the way I figure it, you're rude! You're not only rude, you're ugly!" was my response.

The tall kid's gang snickered, but caught themselves when their leader glared at them. Turning back to me, he snarled, "I'm goin' to bust your face up, Punk. Who do you think you are comin' in here and pushin' yourself around? You ain't dealin' with no wimp here, Man!"

Sizing up the situation, it didn't seem like too much of a challenge to me. I stood back and waited for the kid to swing. When he missed a few punches, I cut loose, and beat the kid to a bloody pulp.

Now I was a winner in more ways than one. Walking smugly away from the fight, with Marilyn wrapped around my arm, I knew I was "in" with his gang too.

Word of my fighting prowess spread quickly. Every one of the White gangs now tried to get me to join them. But my response was always: "I'll think about it. Don't rush me into anything, Man."

But I was always too much of a loner and never did get involved with any gang, even when later on I could have joined the Hell's Angels. I felt safer that way. I knew I could trust myself, but I wasn't so sure about the other guy. I developed a little code to live by: One, you always beat the tar out of the guy who laughs at you; and two, if anyone picks on someone weaker, you help the weaker one.

I reasoned that, regardless of who issued the challenge, it was always right to fight, if you were openly challenged. I loved the sensation of adrenalin pumping through my body during a fight, and I thrived when I spotted fear in an opponent's eyes. I could always recognize fear when his eyes became pinpoints or got very large, by the nervous twitch of his lip and the nervous shuffling of feet.

43

A kid named Jerry came into my life one day when he befriended me in class. Jerry was one of those kids who was a little out of touch with life. He was a real egghead. He was not only overweight, but he had thick, Coke-bottle lenses for glasses. He was known as a "dip," but I liked him. Every day he handed me a notebook, paper, pencil and supplies because I never seemed to remember my own. We became good friends.

One night after school two upper-class gang members caught Jerry in the locker room and beat him unmercifully. Poor Jerry wound up in the hospital with a severe concussion. It wasn't until the next morning in class that I discovered Jerry was in a coma.

Sick on the inside for my friend, I could feel my adrenalin begin to rise. I went to the restroom and vomited. I sat in one of the stalls and wept as the anger boiled inside me. Who would do that to poor Jerry?

The school officials investigated, but came up empty-handed. By quietly poking around and keeping my eyes and ears open, I learned the names of the two ninth-graders who had done it.

I decided to stick close to them and watch for a slip-up. It paid off. A couple of days later, they bragged that they'd nearly killed someone with their bare hands. I bided my time. When Friday came, I got my chance to get even for Jerry.

I didn't even go to class that day. Instead, I went to the gym and got a baseball bat. Then I went to the lavatory, where kids went to smoke, and hid in one of the stalls, smoking one cigarette after another until they showed up. My imagination ran wild, thinking what they'd look like when I got through with them.

It wasn't long before the two ninth-graders pranced

into the lavatory for their smoke. Of course, they didn't know I was only four feet away, hiding in a stall. My feet were up so they couldn't see me. I could hear them joking again about how they put poor Jerry in the hospital.

I couldn't wait any longer. I burst out of the stall and attacked them with the fury of a wild animal—like some sort of street avenger. As the bat swung back, it broke the bathroom mirror. Glass sprayed everywhere. It startled all of us; time seemed to stop momentarily. Then the flurry of blows continued.

The first blow cracked two of the first kid's ribs. He lay there moaning and groaning. The next blow I swung at the kid's head, breaking his jaw in several places. I later remembered it flopping loosely at the bottom of his face.

The other boy screamed in fright and threw his arms up across his face to protect himself. It didn't help. I swung again, dislocating his shoulder. I came at him again, this time shattering his nose. Blood spattered onto the gray floor, with more on the wall. I felt sheer delight and grim satisfaction as I glanced around the room at the havoc I'd caused.

I ran out of the bathroom, flipped the bat in a garbage can and went to class. Meekly, I asked the teacher to excuse me for being late.

"I'm sorry, Mr. Smith, for being late. But, you see, my mother wasn't feeling well this morning, so I decided to stay home a while to give her some help." Then, with an angelic look on my face, I quietly took my seat.

Later that afternoon, I was called to the principal's office. Sure enough, a policeman was waiting. Luckily, I'd already thought through my response if I were questioned about the incident.

In a relaxed manner, I simply told the officer that the

two boys had jumped me in the bathroom. I implied that they had been lying in wait in the bathroom with a bat, and had threatened me with it if I squealed on them.

"I was just lucky, Sir, that I was able to grab the bat from the first kid before he hit me. I guess I just lost my temper and went outta my head in trying to defend myself."

Fortunately for me, they believed my story. After all, who'd believe that a seventh-grader would be crazy enough to take on two ninth-graders? I didn't know it at the time, but Jerry came out of his coma that same day and positively identified the same two boys as his assailants.

The matter was closed and I, once again, felt the delight of not only having taken care of my friend Jerry's attackers single-handedly, but also in pulling the wool over the system's eyes.

* * * * * *

Adolescent years are usually marked by a search for heroes. And I was no different. My real hero was my Uncle Mick—my mom's brother. As an eighth-grader, I wanted to be just like Mick. He was a real con man. He saw life as one big party—one giant poker game filled with bluffing and trickery. I liked the way Mick dressed, kinda "hip" and real sharp. Mick's greatest skill was getting money out of suckers. He knew more ways to do this than I could even count. I sensed that even Pop admired Mick, to some extent.

Once in a while I'd hear Pop say, "I gotta hand it to him. That Mick's a genius. Anyone who can pull the wool over that many people's eyes has gotta be a cut above the rest."

Eighth grade marked the end of my school career. I was bored. I felt like no one cared about me. No one seemed to know what to do. They called me stupid. I knew better; I was smarter than all of them, but I just couldn't read. I had no heart to struggle with school anymore, so I quit.

I began to think about Uncle Mick and to daydream about easy ways to make money, except I wanted to make lots of money. I could see now that Mick was just small-time stuff in the money department. I wanted enough money so I could go to a show anytime I wanted, to buy whatever I wanted and even be able to take Marilyn out on shopping sprees to buy whatever she wanted. My favorite afternoon dream was to visualize turning Marilyn loose in a shopping mall and giving her enough money to buy anything she desired.

Like a lot of junior high kids, I decided to go into the newspaper business. But my friend Doby and I had a different angle. We'd buy one Sunday paper and separate it into single sheets. Then we'd wrap these single sheets around old newspapers that we'd collected from garbage cans. We made a great profit peddling the counterfeit papers from door to door for a full quarter apiece. On a good day, we'd pull in $20 easy.

I figured out the best place to sell papers was at the train depot. It was a great place because the chances were slim of ever seeing the same commuters again. The passengers often paid us with a dollar bill or, sometimes, even a five-dollar bill.

When we were paid with a big bill, we learned to time it so that the train would start pulling away before we got change back to the customer. The train had pulled out of the station before the commuter realized what had happened. It was a double payoff for me. I got a big kick out of watching the angry men yell out the windows of the train as it pulled away, shaking their fists at us—while we held *their* cash in *our* hands. It was one of my greatest joys.

To many of the mine workers, Pop was known as Smiley—a facetious way of pointing out Pop's stern and cantankerous nature. I feared my dad's temper something fierce. In a matter of seconds, I'd often seen Pop go from the heights of joy and laughter to angry rage. Well, the newspaper caper would soon catapult me into one of the most awesome, frightening incidents I would ever experience where Pop's temper was concerned.

One day, Smiley Rearick had a chance conversation with the foreman at the mine, who said sarcastically, "I'm surprised you still work here, Rearick."

"What do you mean?"

"You mean you haven't heard about your boy selling used newspapers down at the train station? With all the dough they're makin', I thought sure you'd retire by now."

Smiley was disgraced before his friends. For all their gruffness and rough ways, they were still honest, hard-working men. Sure, they had problems earning enough money to go around, but they still had honor. I, on the other hand, had violated the code. My dad was humiliated by my thievery.

When I sauntered home that evening, I could see by the look on Pop's face something was very wrong. The belt was already out on the table and Pop was poised for action. The welts on my backside lasted for a week! And that was the end of my brilliant newspaper career. Pop's words, "You ain't *no* good, and you're *never* goin' to be no good either," stung worse than the beating.

Doby and I were real buddies, both seeming to have

the magical touch for mischief. When Doby was dull, I was sharp; when I was dull, Doby was sharp. Actually, we really weren't all that great for each other, but we certainly honed each other's skills for a great career in crime. Our mischief-making at this time, however, was mostly for the sheer fun of it, but the payoffs were great, too.

We became expert at slipping out at night without our folks knowing it. One Saturday night, we hung around the city after curfew, looking for something to do. As we walked by a dark alley, we caught sight of a policeman, so we ducked behind some garbage cans for fear the cop would march us home and turn us in to our folks. If caught, this would mean another belting from Pop. That thought made me sly as a fox.

Peering over the edge of the cans, we were surprised to see the cop raise his nightstick and bash a poor Indian man on the side of his head. He was an old drunk who'd passed out in the alley. While the man lay unconscious, the cop searched him, stuffed all the Indian's valuables in his own pockets and slipped back out onto the street.

We smiled knowingly at each other. *So, even cops are lawbreakers! Everyone's a fake. Uncle Mick's right. Smart guys know how to take advantage of the system and make it pay off for themselves.*

As the cop strolled down the street with the loot in his pockets, a sound caught his ear—the sound of our bumping into a can. Doby started to run, but I sensed something bigger coming down. As the cop turned to chase us, I stepped out into the light.

"Hey, Man, you don't want to bust us. You've got a good deal going. How 'bout forming a partnership?"

I stood with my hands on my hips and a big grin on my face waiting for the cop to reply. Of course, he had no choice but to listen. So, before the night was over, we boys had taken another fateful step into the world of crime. We had formed a new partnership with a cop.

Doby and I proved quickly that we had the guts to do the street work in this venture. We'd watch the street, leaving the cop plenty of time to do the dirty work on the alley drunks. Though he kept most of the spoils, we turned a pretty good profit. At the tender age of 13, Doby and I spent that entire summer in the business of helping to roll drunks!

By summer's end, most of the town had heard the rumbles about the hapless drunks being robbed in alleys. None of the partners-in-crime guessed that our "enterprise" was about to come to a screeching halt. One Saturday night, one of the drunks turned out to be a police officer in disguise. Because the Indians had complained often enough about being rolled, the authorities were finally forced to do something about it. So they used a ruse to smoke out the culprits.

As we watched the street this particular night, our cop partner rolled what appeared to be a drunken Indian. Suddenly, the policeman in disguise jumped up and collared the dishonest cop. At the same time, Doby and I were nailed against the wall by plainclothesmen.

Immediately, the three of us were taken to the Los Angeles County Jail and booked. Officer Hunter, our accomplice, later received a swift and harsh sentence. In fact, his case was so publicized many wondered if the dishonest cop would even get a fair trial. Because Hunter was an officer of the law and had committed felonious crimes involving two minors, he was sentenced to 55 years in the California State Pen.

Doby and I were detained at the Juvenile Center,

where they kept kids charged with anything from car theft to murder. The major recreation at the Juvenile Center was fighting. Here I acquired an even greater taste for this low form of sport. I also learned several new, dirty fighting moves that I figured would become important to me when I was sprung.

By 13, my emotional life had become a jumbled mess. I couldn't seem to reconcile my emotional feelings with my outside meanness, which I consistently expressed in unacceptable forms. My own ethical system had to be sorted out. I'd think, "Why was it wrong for those two ninth-graders to beat up Jerry, the egghead, yet it's perfectly okay for me to take from drunks?" I finally came up with my own brand of reasoning on what the difference was: The drunks were adults and should have known better than to pass out in alleys, especially with money in their pockets.

I had one desperate cry I kept burying deeper and deeper in my heart: I wanted so desperately to be loved. But the more trouble I got into, the less Pop would have to do with me. Mom was loving enough towards me—even more so, it seemed, when I got into trouble. However, a teenage boy hungers to hear his dad say, "I love you, Son."

When word filtered down to me about the cop's sentence, I was stunned. "Fifty-five years?! Man, I'll be in here 'til I'm 18, at that rate!"

The prospect of spending another four years in this Juvenile Center frightened me, so I set my mind's goal to control my fear and to make the best of my new surroundings.

I had already established myself as one of the "tough dudes," so life there became fairly safe for me. In addition,

I'd become somewhat of a folk hero, because Mom had talked the Center's authorities into letting her bring a big chocolate cake into the cell section where Doby and I had been assigned. The other guys couldn't believe it. Here's this dude in the slammer for stealing from bums and his mom brings him a chocolate cake. Far out! I was a real winner in their eyes.

I got lucky. When the date for my trial came up, I got a judge who was very sympathetic toward youths. When the crime descriptions were read off, the judge's head shot up upon hearing that it was a crooked cop who involved me in the summer crime spree.

By the start of the following summer, I was back on the street. I had arrived home just in time to pack up for another move of the Rearick clan. This time we ended up in Farmington, New Mexico. Pop's new dream was to be near the oil fields and uranium mines. The whole family had long since lost any hope that a new job would bring any newfound joy to our home.

After the trouble in Colton, I was glad to be able to "cool out" in a smaller town. As I'd earned the respect of the kids of the other miners, I made friends quickly.

* * * * * *

At 14, I was already streetwise. I decided to join the National Guard training camp for two weeks. Because I was so muscular and tough-looking, I easily passed for a 16-year-old, if not an 18-year-old.

I was to report to El Paso, Texas, just minutes from the Mexican border. I fell in quickly with some other young toughs and we decided to spend our evenings in Juárez, Mexico, just over the border. For just a few bucks, a guy could buy a great time in Juárez. The booze was cheap and there were plenty of gals.

It was easy to slip out under the tent each night. Several of us met at a patch of sagebrush. Then, quietly slipping through the streets of El Paso, we'd head for Juárez.

A couple of negative things happened to me while there. I got terrible hangovers from the cheap booze; and, one night, I almost got switchbladed when I put my arm around the wrong "lady of the night." Lucky for me that her Mexican lover was too drunk to move on me quick enough.

When I returned from the training camp, my folks had packed up again and moved to Moab, Utah. Moab was like a frontier town out of a TV Western. The buildings were wood-framed and dilapidated. As we approached the town, it seemed to rise out of nowhere in the midst of the sandy prairie. Tumbleweeds actually blew across the streets— just like in the movies.

Moab was considered the final stop for miners on a downward spiral. They were the rowdiest bunch I'd ever seen. The saloons were plagued with brawls and fighting around the clock. Often there were stabbings and shootings.

* * * * * *

By 1955, Smiley Rearick was drinking more than ever and his bursts of temper and violence became more frequent. None of us felt safe anymore.

That was the year, I decided to make a big announcement: No more school! Mom gave in quickly. She instinctively knew I'd be in class for only a few days anyway before I'd be expelled again.

Pop was drinking when I announced this. He turned his flushed face and bloodshot eyes towards me and slurred out a command, "Then, from now on, you're on your own. If you're goin' to sleep under my roof, you can come to work in the mines like the rest of us!"

"Fine!" I barked back.

I snagged a job at the uranium mine, running a jackhammer. And I could hold my own with the best of them. In fact, I could work faster and harder than many of the men who'd been there for years. I decided, however, that I wasn't going to stay long in this sweat trap. Pop had worked himself to the bone like some sleazy animal for a lot of years, and it'd gotten him nothing, so I wasn't about to fall into the same rut.

My youthful energy took me into bars for many late nights of drinking beer and card playing. Pop chuckled about this, thinking it would be great to be young again.

My favorite hangout was the Bluebird Saloon. There was always a great poker game going on in the back room—a secret game because gambling was illegal in Moab. I loved to watch the game after the owner finally trusted me enough to let me in. I never played, though, because the stakes were way too high for me.

One night, a dealer from Salt Lake City was accused of cheating. Thereupon, one of the gruff miners snatched a pistol from inside his boot, put it to the dealer's head and growled, "You cheatin' so-and-so! Gimme back my money or I'll blow your head off!"

Jake, the owner, coolly took the gun from the miner's hand as he slid piles of money back to each player. Everyone breathed a sigh of relief, but the game broke up for the night, leaving the dealer completely unnerved by the incident. After everyone left, I heard him declare, "That does it! I quit, Jake! You've got a bunch of madmen in this place!"

I seized the opportunity. "Can *I* try dealin' tomorrow night, Jake?" I blurted out as the owner returned to the room.

"Well, okay, Ron. Sure. You're on! I ain't got no one else anyway. If you deal for me tomorrow night, I'll pay ya $75."

The next night, I began my career as a card dealer. I made a good game of it too, which really pleased Jake. I livened up the game with humorous one-liners—a little levity here and there—and seemed to be good at egging on the bets, especially in a tense game.

I mused, "Poor Pop! He labors all day long in the mine for peanuts, compared to this!"

* * * * * *

By the time I turned 15, my daily earnings were three times what Smiley Rearick made in the mines. Of course, my mining career came to a screeching halt when I started card-dealing.

I practically lived at the Bluebird Saloon. I became a superb pool player and could hold my drinks as good as any adult. I could even hold my own in a fight, if the need arose. And with my new card-dealing career, I had plenty of dough to boot. Rarely did I go home; when I got hungry, I simply walked across the street to Rose's Cafe and ordered the best meal in town.

At Rose's Cafe, the waitress and the cook were one and the same. Clarissa was 21, half-Mexican, half-Indian and incredibly beautiful. She took a liking to me, laughed a lot, knew how to tease and was an exceptionally good listener. For the first time in my life, I found myself talking for hours on end to another human being.

To my disappointment, however, Clarissa was married. Her husband worked the night shift at the mine seven days a week.

"I'm a very lonely woman," Clarissa confided one night.

Of course, I knew what she meant by that, and I found it increasingly harder to stay away from Rose's Cafe. I started to plot how I could possibly ask a married woman out. Even if I did, where would we go?

Late one Monday night, no one showed up at Jake's to play Black Jack, so I eagerly walked across the street and ordered a steak, so I could be near Clarissa. I started to blurt out that I'd like to take her someplace classy. But even before I finished the sentence, she whispered for me to come to her apartment, upstairs.

This clandestine relationship lasted six months. Never once did I divulge my age to Clarissa, because I knew she was several years older than I and thought she might laugh at me if she knew my true age. Because I loved her so much, I didn't seem to pick up on the fact that though I told her repeatedly I loved her, she never returned the same sentiment. One day, I begged her to run away with me and become my wife. She turned me down. Though stung by this rebuff, I still continued the relationship.

One evening, I learned that Clarissa had been badly beaten by her husband. For days I seethed with anger over it, and sat around the bar trying to figure out how I could get a gun to gun him down. It seems that Clarissa's husband had found a man's watch, which he knew belonged to his boss, in their apartment. Clarissa, when discovered, haughtily replied she had been "entertaining" many nighttime "guests."

Many nighttime guests? When she knew I loved her? How could she! I fumed a long time over this startling information. The word *many* became branded on my mind and heart, as though put there by a smoldering iron.

You idiot, Ron. How could you let yourself get in a place where you trusted a woman! You've never been able to trust any man, so what made you think you could trust a woman? Why did you believe Clarissa's affections and all her loving words? What a fool you've been, Ron!

My view of women immediately took a turn for the worse that evening. I sat, smoking one cigarette after another, gulping down beer after beer.

I'll never trust anyone again. The way I figure it, you gotta take care of yourself. I'll never get caught like this again . . . not by any babe . . . not by any sleaze bag like that!

6

A Cold Heart

Clarissa ended up leaving town, and I continued my job as dealer at the Bluebird Saloon.

I felt the need to pay my way, so I took some of my earnings home to Mom. But most of my money was eaten up by drinking and gambling. Already, at only 15, I was becoming as much of an alcoholic as Pop was.

Besides the great pay I got for dealing cards at Jake's, I decided to develop several other "enterprises" so I could pick up some extra dough. I got hold of an acquaintance who regularly needed cash so he could import prostitutes. For a piece of the action, I let him have money and became part owner of the only prostitution establishment in Moab.

When there wasn't enough cash to get by on, I didn't think twice about dipping into Jake's till. I figured Jake owed me anyway. After all, I was the bouncer for the joint too. Didn't I have it comin' to me? I rationalized, "What the heck! Jake makes real good money anyway. No reason he shouldn't share some of it with me."

Because of my reputation for fighting, I didn't get much peace in a little town like Moab. It got so I couldn't even play a game of pool or darts without someone trying to turn the game into a brawl. Even total strangers would enter the bar and curse at me, just to get me riled up.

At those times, I'd almost go crazy with anger. After all, I sure had a good teacher in Pop on how to unleash fury and hatred in an instant. I'd never been a clean fighter either. Why fight at all if you don't plan to come out on top?

By now, I'd become quite ruthless. I'd use a pool stick, a broken bottle or whatever else I could lay my hands on to make certain I won over an opponent. Once a brawl began, all reason left me; I had only one goal: to destroy— or even kill, if need be—my opponent.

My commitment to the underdog was fading quickly, for I now felt that mercy was just a sign of weakness. My acquaintances no longer viewed me as just a tough guy, but as someone truly dangerous, someone to be very careful around.

Smiley and Opal Rearick began hearing stories about what the town thought of their son Ronny. Repeatedly Pop came to me, making clumsy attempts to try to redirect me into less violent ways, but it usually ended up in an angry exchange of words. To me it was needling. Besides, Pop was never good at expressing himself.

Our angry exchanges always ended by Pop saying, "You're no good and you're never goin' to amount to anything! I've known it all your life. Ron Rearick, you're just no good! You're never goin' to amount to anything!"

Pop's words were always like a knife being driven through my heart. I soon began to believe those hotly spoken words. I felt I was no good and wouldn't amount to anything. That really scared me!

Smiley and Opal Rearick decided to leave Moab; they moved up to Salt Lake City. I felt I needed a change too, so two pals and I decided to journey across the country—sort of a driving tour, with no particular destination or goal in mind. The night we left, I dipped once more into Jake's cash supply as a sort of farewell bonus, waved good-bye to my card-dealing job and headed south.

"Where we goin'?" one of the guys asked.

"There's a million places to see. Let's see all we can," I replied.

"Aren't we goin' to have to stop and work along the way?"

"Naw, we can steal whatever we need."

Our cross-country vacation actually turned into a cross-country crime spree. We robbed our way through Utah, Nevada and Arizona, all the way into the heart of Texas, then back up to Oklahoma, drinking and brawling our way through dozens of small towns. We felt invincible. The guys on the TV series "Route 66" were our heroes.

As most of our heists were small, we managed to keep ahead of the law. The only time we ended up in the slammer was for drunk driving. We really sweated it out that weekend because, under the backseat of the car, was a treasure chest of loose change that Chad Barker, one of the three "vacationers," had extracted from cigarette and pop machines along the way. Lee Williams, the third member of this illustrious band, and I spent the whole weekend telling Chad to keep his cool. As luck would have it, the car was never searched and we were out the following Monday.

After several months of this riotous living, we were not only tired of being on the road, but fed up with each other as well. When my cousin Jack invited me to share his apartment for a few weeks, I jumped at it, thinking it'd be a welcome relief and give me the solitude I needed for a while. Besides, Chad and Lee were such maniacs. I was sure they were bound to get in big trouble before long anyway and I didn't want to be around when it happened.

Jack worked for a company in Oklahoma that ran oil rigs. I asked Jack if he could get me on the payroll; within a week I was working. Those were good months in my life. The oil riggers were tough but hard-working, and they quickly took me in as one of them. For the first time in many years, I began to feel normal.

I could really turn on the charm when I wanted to and become an extrovert real quick if I figured there was something in it for me. As long as no one discovered I couldn't read or write, I was okay.

It surprised me to learn that the oil workers not only cussed, drank and gambled as well as I could, but were also quite settled down with wives and families. I began cultivating thoughts that, maybe, this was the life for me too. I could stay in one place and keep the same friends for the rest of my life, and have a good time besides.

Then I met Anna. Anna was very striking—tall and slender, the kind I liked. Her Scandinavian heritage showed in her finely chiseled features and long, blond hair.

I had gone alone to a local dance; Anna had come with another oil worker. We caught each other's eye across the dance floor, had a few dances together, and Anna left with me. Though her Scandinavian background gave her a cool, sophisticated look, she had a great sense of humor. She'd have a good time at parties, but never really liked to drink with me. Instead, she was more interested in impressing me with her cooking abilities. I sure had some great meals at the Sorenson home.

One day on the job, I recounted to Jack the great meal I'd had the night before at Anna's.

"Jack, you wouldn't believe how thick that steak was! We also had baked potatoes with sour cream and chives. That was some meal, Jackie. I'm tellin' ya, Anna's sure a good cook."

Jack looked up from his tuna fish sandwich. "Ronny, you know why she's fixin' you those meals?"

"No. Why?"

"Wake up, Ron. Any woman who starts cookin' up for ya wants to marry ya. You oughtta ask her, Ron. She'd make a great little woman."

I didn't reply, but it sure got me to thinking. *After all, Anna's a real classy gal. And it's gettin' kinda old livin' on Jack's couch. Why not get married? I've already sown my share of wild oats. Eighteen's old enough to get married. Besides, I'd make a great husband! And I'm tired of pickin' up chicks at bars, tired of these chicks who can't even remember your last name when they see ya next. Besides, these one-night stands are gettin' old. I'm tired of worrying about catchin' some VD. By golly, that sounds like a good idea.*

So in March 1959 Anna and I tied the knot. We eloped.

"Look at me!" I exclaimed, grinning at Anna as we drove across the Oklahoma plains on our honeymoon. "Ron Rearick, the all-American guy, has a job, car payments and a new wife—and a beautiful new wife you are!"

I liked living a normal life and did quite well at it for a while. But nothing had really changed. We started fighting—occasionally at first, then more and more often, followed by times of passionate love-making. Within the year, Kathy was born. After the baby came, though, married life got tough on me. Kathy was about six months old when I first noticed that she was getting on my nerves.

On top of that, Anna complained constantly. She was always nagging at me to stop smoking and drinking. This really burned me up. After all, I thought I was doing real good by cutting way back on both, and I hardly ever gambled anymore.

I grew restless. I returned to the bars and gambling—only on weekends, though. Monday through Thursday nights, I did my drinking at home. But Friday, Saturday and Sunday nights, I partied, leaving Anna and little Kathy alone at home to fend for themselves.

By the second year, our marriage was one endless fight. I yelled at Anna; she screamed back. Often, I hit her. Little Kathy's crying didn't help; it kept me constantly on edge. Though she was a pretty baby, my own daughter didn't fill my heart with the love I expected to feel for her.

Life became a giant disappointment. Women drove me nuts. My own wife drove me nuts. And now my own little girl drove me nuts. Why should I keep on trying anyway? I decided then that this normal life was no longer for me.

So I decided that my marriage would be better off if I returned to my old self. Of course, being my old self meant bar-hopping, stealing and fighting.

One Tuesday night, I drove to the neighboring town of Norman, Oklahoma, for a hot game of poker. By now, I was a card expert. However, that particular night, some turkey from Reno was picking up every hand. I'd been paid $70 that day for working on the rigs, and I lost it all to the guy from Reno. I knew Anna was counting on that money for groceries. I felt rotten, and desperate.

Man, I thought. *I can't go back to Anna without the money, and I know Kathy needs some milk. What'll I do?*

I began to calculate how I could regain the lost money

and get back home. I also wondered how the Reno dude had been able to play so well. I'd carried a gun hidden under the front seat of my car for quite some time—ever since my cross-country crime spree with Lee and Chad. As I wildly drove down the freeway, I reached down to see if it was still there. It was—loaded and ready.

I pulled off the freeway and headed towards the first market I spotted. It was a small grocery store—the Mom and Pop type—on a little country road, with late-night hours. The elderly owners were just closing up for the night when I strode in. They both looked up to greet me, then froze at the sight of my gun.

I barked, "Open the register and give me the money, and no one will get hurt!"

"Yes, Sonny," the old man said fearfully. His hands shook as he opened the register, scooped everything out of the till and handed it to me in a paper bag.

I could tell when I glanced into the bag there was at least $200, more than enough to replace the grocery money I'd lost gambling. I turned to leave, but another idea came to me. A store this far from the bank usually had a safe. If so, that would really make this stop worthwhile! I grabbed the old man and held the revolver to his head.

"Now, let's go to the safe, old man!"

The old man's wife blurted out in a terrified voice, "Tell him, Daddy! Tell him where it is. It's okay, Daddy. We'll get it back."

Pointing behind the shelf containing shampoos and hair sprays, the old man croaked, "There! Behind there!"

The old woman frantically pushed the cans aside and worked the safe's combination. The safe door swung open. Wow! I'd hit it big! The safe was filled with money from several weeks' earnings. I began scooping piles of bills into a large grocery bag.

But a strange thing happened to me when I stood up after emptying the safe. I looked from the old man to the old woman, who were obviously heartbroken. They reached for each other's hands in a comforting way.

The old man spoke. "Son, you're too smart to have to treat people this way to get money. God has a better plan for you."

There they were, old, weak and so vulnerable. *What am I doin' pickin' on these poor old people? I've really sunk low.*

I handed the bag of money back to the old man. "Here you go, Pop. I'm not going to steal it all. Just count out $70, the grocery money I lost tonight gambling. My kid's sick and my wife's hungry. I just need my grocery money, that's all."

Smiling, but with shaking hands, the old man counted out $70, then said, "There's a better way, Son."

I stuffed the money in my shirt pocket and strode out the door. I glanced back at them, spat on the ground and hollared, "Don't you dare call the cops either, or I'll come back here and find ya, and you'll both be dead!"

As I hurried from the store, the old man shouted after me, "We're going to be praying for you, Son. Every day!"

The money felt like lead in my pocket, and my heart ached because of what I'd done to those poor old folks.

7

Seventh Avenue in Oakland

"Stealin' money from old people just ain't my game!" I said to myself. "This bend-in-the-road town is driving me nuts! Look what it's makin me do! I need to get some city life, some excitement. Yep, that's what I need."

To Anna, I said, "Anna, start packing! We're movin' to Oakland, California!"

We left the next day. Anna was more in favor of the move than I'd expected. It hadn't dawned on me that she'd be closer to her father, Thor Sorenson. As soon as we got to town, Anna was all over her folks, crying and telling them how mean I was and how bad I'd been treating her and Kathy.

The change of scenery didn't improve our marriage as I'd hoped. The last straw came when Thor came over one evening. Shaking his fist in my face, his own face getting redder by the minute, he hollered accusingly, "Ron, you're not treating my Anna and my Kathy like you should! I'll not stand for my grandbaby being treated like this! And you're *no good* for my darling Anna either! You're just *no good*, Ronald Rearick! You're *no good!* You'll *never* be any good!"

Thor's accusations had a very familiar ring to them. I'd heard these same words so many times before. Once again, the harsh words drove like a stake through my heart. Pop had said the very same things to me, over and over again, "Ron, you're *no good* . . . and you're *never* goin' to amount to anything either!"

It was like a broken record. As usual, when faced with these searing, taunting words, my only impulse was to run. In a cold, emotionless voice, I told Anna good-bye. Then I turned to Thor and stated coldly, "All right, then you take care of them from now on!"

Turning on my heel, I walked out the door, feeling sure I'd never see them again.

* * * * * *

The area around Seventh Avenue in Oakland had my kind of people. Immediately I landed a job as a bouncer at the Top Hat Nightclub. Pointing to my thick arms and big fists, the owner said, "With 'guns' like those, you ought to be able to handle any of the flakes we get in here. We'll call you 'Mr. Enforcer.'"

I loved this profession. "Legal" violence was great! And the respect I gained really bolstered my ego. I loved being around these people and knew how to handle the nightlife. Hell's Angels were probably the best party people I'd known.

It was in a topless joint on Broadway where I met Sandy, a great dancer. She was well endowed and a real find as far as I was concerned. She wasn't shy about letting me know that her sexual talent was not her only ability either; she also claimed to be a thief extraordinaire.

Before long, we were off on a crime spree together. I

really liked Sandy, though she scared me a little; from time to time her criminal prowess was almost supernatural.

At first, we hit mostly jewelry stores up and down the California coast. I wanted to know what our method of operation was to be for our first job.

Sandy grinned. "I have an ingenious MO, if you want to call it that. You pretend you're my fiancé. When we go into a jewelry store, you ask to see a tray of diamonds, then look at me with a starry-eyed gaze. While we're look-ing at the rings, there'll be two friends outside starting a fake brawl. Usually what happens then is the store man-ager gets distracted and sends a couple of employees out to break up the fight. Do you follow me?"

"Yep, loud and clear."

"So, there we are with the tray of rings in front of us. After that, it's simple. You take the fakes out of your pocket and exchange them for those on the tray. When the fight's over, we tell the clerk that we're going home to talk it over. Then we leave. A great scheme, huh?"

It seemed like a great plan all right, and foolproof. We could make thousands a week! The best part of the MO was that it would be hard to spot anything missing from the tray. The missing rings could go unnoticed for hours. In fact, it could even be days before other customers wanted to look at the same tray. By that time, I would have the diamonds reset by my connection and disposed of. And we'd have plenty of money in our pockets. It was a great setup!

* * * * * *

In the early '60s, the Bay Area was just starting to get loaded up with drugs. First I acquired a taste for marijuana and then several varieties of pills. I embraced drugs with the same wreckless abandon I did fighting. My drug habit escalated so quickly that it took several jewelry robberies just to keep me supplied.

My first love became high-grade cocaine. A snort of coke made me feel like a king; I felt invincible; I felt like *somebody*. I also became a connoisseur of good marijuana, or weed, the stuff from South America being my preference. But I always returned to coke. Coke and a good gal like Sandy could keep me going forever.

I began meeting some guys who called themselves acid heads. "What's an 'acid head'?" I wanted to know.

"Hey, Man, I like to fly on LSD," one of them replied.

Not many had heard of LSD in those days, but it was beginning to be passed around rather freely in the bars around Oakland. I tried it a couple of times, but decided I was a coke man. The only problem was: Coke wasn't cheap, and it was definitely more than a bouncer could afford.

A funny thing happens in the mind of a thief driven by a heavy dope habit: The money and belongings of others become your own—almost like the fruit of the land. It was easy for me to adapt to this kind of philosophy. I felt I could "borrow" anything I needed, as long as it kept my habit going. After all, I figured, if I had a bundle of dough or things to give away, I'd sure give them to *my* friends.

I made friends with a biker named Frenchy Peterson, who tried desperately to sign me up with the Hell's Angels. But I never did. I sure liked their parties, though. Those Angels sure knew how to throw a good party!

From the time I met Frenchy, I never spent a weekend alone. The Angels received me as one of their own, even though I wasn't a "member in good standing." I was known as a "non-member in good standing." I lived out every fantasy you could imagine. My life became one gigantic drug and sex orgy.

Sandy and I soon moved in together. One day, quite by accident, we learned that our neighbor, Mr. Cole, ordered pharmaceutical supplies for drugstores. One afternoon, in late October 1962, I decided we could hit this guy hard for a load of dope. Then we could throw the greatest party anyone around there had ever seen.

"Sandy, Cole must have thousands of uppers and downers. We're talkin' about hostin' a real party!"

It took us a couple of days to lay down our plan, which we finalized over a couple of lines of great coke the night before the heist was to come down. We waited until the next morning when Cole got into his car. Then I, who was hiding on the floor of the backseat, simply sat up and put a sawed-off shotgun to the back of Cole's head. Cole, of course, started shaking and babbling; he begged me not to kill him.

My instinct told me that the guy didn't even carry a piece to protect his stuff. *Imagine, this guy's got all this dope and no gun!*

I got out of the car, took the key, opened up the trunk, took the trays of drugs out, leaned through the window on the passenger side and said, "If you turn and look to see who we are, I'll blow your brains out!"

We were ecstatic. Sandy spent most of the evening inviting everyone we knew to the party that weekend. By the next morning, the word was out: Booze and pills were "on the house" at Rearick's place.

I didn't know at the time that this party would be the end of my Seventh Avenue days. Two biker groups and a variety of street people showed up. Every kind of person imaginable came and the music was blasting the whole neighborhood away; motorcycles were lined up and down the street for blocks. It was obvious that a very noisy, boisterous party was in session.

It took 12 ice chests to hold all the booze we'd bought for the party. Cole's pills were set up like a smorgasbord so everyone could serve themselves, buffet-style. We didn't have to label them because this crowd was sharp enough to know what they were taking, just by the color and shape of the pills.

It was inevitable that the cops would eventually come. The noise got so loud from all the laughter and carrying-on in the house and the bikers zooming up and down the street that several carloads of reinforcements came to make the bust.

The cops were astounded! They had obviously stumbled onto one of the biggest drug parties ever reported. They ordered the paddy wagon.

Three cops charged the front door and kicked it in. About six others jumped over the back fence. Chicks and bikers scattered in all directions. A few of the hippie types just sat still, obviously stoned, out in the ozone level, on psychedelic drugs. Some of the bikers were still coherent enough to stand their ground and fight the cops, pulling out chains and clubs.

Frenchy, some of the other party goers and I were tossed into the paddy wagon, which was made of heavy metal. We were separated from the cops by a steel mesh screen.

I got real mad and boiled with anger. I'd had enough coke to believe that I could take on anything and anyone.

"Just who do these pigs think they are, crashing my party?!"

Looking out of the wagon, I saw one of the cops smash a downed biker on the head with a billy club. "That does it!" I hollered.

With that, I pushed back against the seat, lifted my legs, and with one, mighty lunge, kicked the side wall out of the paddy wagon. It popped off with a loud crack and came crashing down on the heads of some of the cops. Immediately, the other prisoners leaped out and ran free.

Still seething with rage, I reached up, grabbed the driver by the throat and started choking him, and almost snuffed out his life before two other cops pulled me off.

I was charged with possession of narcotics and received a stiff sentence. I knew I was in for even more punishment when I was told the next day, after I came off my coke high, that I'd wrecked a paddy wagon besides. Cops don't like anyone wrecking their equipment.

On the day of sentencing, I left the courtroom, cuffed and shackled. I was on my way to do eight years at the "gladiator school"—the state pen at Tracy, California.

8

I-C-E

I learned the ropes quickly. Though I'd done county jail time before, this prison was a whole new ball game. However, I caught on quick and learned fast how to get "comfortable."

One day at a time—that's the only way you learn to handle prison life. There's a type of claustrophobia that is experienced only in the state pen. The panic derived from this fear is especially acute for first-timers. I beat this phobia working out with weights and watching baseball games. And it helped a lot when I could find dope in the exercise yard so I could stay high.

Quickly too, I learned to discern the character of other inmates and became an expert at sizing them up. I soon mastered the three cardinal rules of prison life: You hear nothing, you see nothing and, above all, you tell nothing.

The racial fights were tough for me to handle; I hadn't been around many Blacks or Chicanos since living in Colton and hadn't really given much thought to racial matters since. But in prison I had to in order to survive. I was pretty sure I could handle anyone on a one-to-one basis, but the race gangs were mind-boggling, even to a top fighter like myself. It was scary stuff in this prison called Tracy.

My sentence was eight years on the charges of: carrying a deadly weapon, destroying public property, attempting to kill, obstructing an arresting officer, assaulting an officer and possessing narcotics.

It seems that my reputation as a cop fighter had preceded me to Tracy; the correction officers ran me through the hoops right off. I learned another valuable lesson real quick: If you just take their jabs, it will eventually stop.

Tracy was no different than any other prison when it came to its inner structure. It was established by the pecking order of the prisoners. I was tried right off, that is, put to the test.

Some clown came up to me in the chow line, deliberately bumped into me, then pretended it was an accident in such a way that it was obvious it really wasn't. The tray flew from my hands and food splashed all over the floor. Plastic plates bounced with a clatter, and my knife and fork clanged to the floor. Everyone looked at me and grinned, waiting to see what I was made of.

I kept my cool, even when the guy gave a phony apology. The cops in the room just watched because they also knew what was coming down. Anyway, they really couldn't do too much about it after the fact.

It was obviously showdown time, and it was all on my shoulders now. I just grinned back and said, "Hey, Man, no sweat." Then I walked to the back of the line, got another tray of food and headed over for coffee.

I took my time as I lifted my coffee cup from under the spout of the coffee dispenser, sipping a little of the hot coffee and watching guardedly where the guy who'd bumped into me sat down. I could tell the guy was part of a small elite group. This was their way of letting me know who was "in charge" and that I'd better not mess with them.

Sauntering over to their table and acting as though I'd tripped, I emptied the whole cup of hot coffee onto the dude's lap!

"Oops! Excuse me!" I said in mock sympathy as I walked on to another table and sat down. Everyone laughed. I'd made my point; I wasn't afraid of anyone—not even these three "someones."

The inmates were given about a half-hour of shower time each night. That night, as usual, I grabbed my towel and headed for the changing area. I hung my pants and shirt on the rack outside the stall, carefully put my shoes with my socks stuffed in them on the rack above the hangers, put my shorts on the hook under my pants and entered the shower room.

As I was about to enter a stall, I noticed some of the guys left, leaving me alone with the guy involved in the tray/coffee incident earlier that day. Then I noticed that another of the punks from the same table was there. I figured he was the lookout to spot any guards.

Instinctively I knew what was coming down: They were going to rape me! In prison, rape is an act of violence, an attempt to dehumanize another. I thought, *Fat chance I'll let them get me!*

I yelled out loud, "Come on, fagots, come and get it! Come on! Let's see if you can take me on!"

The bigger of the two lunged at me. I grabbed him around the neck and popped him real good in both eyes and nose. Blood spurted onto the dressing bench. Then a third, smaller guy ran at me. I hadn't seen him before. He must have been hiding around the corner by the lockers.

Quick as a wink, I kicked the third guy in the groin, then turned to keep track of the other fighter. The shorter one had been slowed down some, but not stopped. As I hung onto the first guy's neck, I kicked repeatedly at the little guy.

I was holding them all off pretty good when the guy watching the door joined in. I knew I had to act fast if I were going to come out of this OK. Without thinking, I immediately gouged an eye out of the guy whose head I still held in a vise-like grip. It just hung there grotesquely, about one-and-a-half inches out on the dude's cheek, with only its internal fibers holding it.

Everything came to a screeching halt. The injured guy passed out. I yelled, "Come any closer and I'll pull the thing right outta his head!"

The other would-be assailants turned and walked out without a word. I moved the injured guy over beside one of the benches, took a shower, dressed and left. No one "saw" anything, "heard" anything or "said" anything. The dude just had an "accident."

This story spread like wildfire among the young cons. One of the guys, who had been in on the shower-room incident, later said to me: "Man, that was ice!"

Another, who heard the story, exclaimed, "Hell! He's the Iceman!"

After that, my next two-and-a-half years were halfway decent. I liked the new name. It had a nice ring to it. I was "Iceman." I was someone to be reckoned with—and no one would mess with me now.

9

The Army—Failure to Adjust

After two-and-a-half years, I was eligible for parole, so I decided to return to Salt Lake City and try my luck there. I rented an apartment and spent several days just lying in the sun. I couldn't stand to stay indoors more than an hour or so before I'd start to get edgy. It was hard to sleep at night because I kept having recurrent dreams about being sent back to the pen.

I'd been out of prison only a few weeks when a draft notice came from Uncle Sam. The United States Army wanted me. Because prison life had calmed me down, I made it satisfactorily through boot camp. Following boot camp at Ford Ord, we spent several weeks at Fort Dix, fully expecting to be sent off to Korea. But to the surprise of the entire company, my outfit was sent to Germany instead.

Upon landing in northern Germany, I was awed by the winter landscape. After my time in the pen, the snow-covered hillsides of Germany reminded me more than ever of my days in Wrightwood. The snow there, however, had been confined to a single mountain where I'd taken ski lessons. I loved that winter and how the snow blended all the landscapes together.

In April the snow began to melt and everything seemed gray again. A sense of uneasiness overtook me, which I hadn't experienced since my last few days with Anna and Kathy.

Routine army life quickly became boring because a guy could only party on weekends or when on leave. It didn't take long, however, to discover that American goods—easily available on the base—brought high prices in the German villages. So my boredom soon passed, as I managed to keep busy developing my own Black Market.

GIs could buy cigarettes in the PX for $1.50 a carton and sell them in town for $5! A pint of whiskey cost $2.75 on the base, but I could turn around and sell it for a whopping $35 on the German streets! Black Marketeers made huge profits on anything and everything, from warm winter clothing to gasoline. I soon became very adept at this "profession."

The Vietnam War was just beginning to hit the papers back home. Lieutenants, looking for volunteers for that war, were a regular sight on the bases in those days. The lieutenant went on and on about the extra pay and early discharges being handed out to those who volunteered for Vietnam duty. I couldn't believe all the turkeys who signed up for a tour of duty in Nam. I thought they were nuts. I figured I'd been through my share of wars and it was safer to stay right there in Germany. Besides, I had a good, cushiony life in Germany. Why give it up to fight in a place I'd never heard of before?

Some of the PX goods could be purchased only with ration cards, so I devised a scheme so I could collect dozens of ration cards besides mine, and cornered the loan shark market. A loan shark in the army provided money to guys who needed it—very short term at very high interest!

By the time I arrived at Wieldflichen, there was already a well-established loan shark. This dude would loan $10, but required $20 in return—double what he had loaned. I checked him out and figured I could handle him easily enough, even if things got physical. So, my own loan business began by loaning out $10, but requiring only $15 in return. As expected, it wasn't long before the competition's anger was stirred up.

One night, a hulk of a sergeant cornered me in the chow line. Clenching his fist under my nose and glaring into my eyes, he growled, "Look, Buster, this ain't no backwoods operation. If you want your head busted open, just make one more loan! Got it?"

"Sure, Man. I understand," I answered slowly, stretching my lips into a phony smile.

This wasn't the time to lay into the guy, particularly as I didn't intend to serve any time in the brig on account of him or anybody else. So, I decided I'd catch this guy when he wasn't looking.

The opportunity came that very night. I found Sergeant Rayburn all alone in a bar in town. I sneaked up behind him, grabbed him and punched him around. Though Rayburn was much heavier than I, he didn't know how to handle dirty fighting. It was all over in a few moments. Picking the sergeant up by his lapels, I heaved him through the bar's plate glass window. His limp body hit the sidewalk at the feet of another GI.

"Hey, Mister, did you drop something?" the GI asked.

"I guess I did," I answered, laughing.

That was the beginning of a friendship that would last for many years. The GI was Stubs Reilly—soulmate and soon-to-be partner in my loan shark business. Of course, as soon as I cornered the market, I raised the interest rate to 100 percent. If the GIs couldn't pay, they had to fork over their ration cards.

* * * * * *

In the early 1960s, the German society was no more prepared for the drug culture than the American society was. I proceeded to introduce Stubs to the adventures of the drug world. Together, we saw still another opportunity for yet another great business venture as the drug scene caught on at the army bases of Europe.

Hashīsh, or hash, was plentiful in Germany, with most of the drugs coming in from Holland and the high-grade dope from Amsterdam. Stubs and I got most of our drug stock by trading base whiskey for it. Eventually, we tapped into the real hot line of heroin—where the big money was on the bases.

Stubs and I put in most of our army time hanging around the bars for hours on end. One day, while killing time in a bar, Stubs discovered that my nickname was Iceman.

"Man, that really fits, because you are cold!"

Stubs had already witnessed my ruthless nature on a number of occasions. Thereafter, I was known all over camp as Iceman.

Army sergeants, to me, were just as obnoxious as any other authority figure I'd had to deal with in my life, and I had no use for them at all. I especially hated the stupid war games we were forced to participate in. Every sergeant seemed to become a little Napoleon when out in the field.

In October 1964, our battalion was ordered out on field maneuvers. Here we were, thousands of soldiers, out "playing war." My stockpile of cash meant virtually nothing out on the field. I, like all the other soldiers, spent most of my time on my hands and knees, crawling under brier bushes through mud, trying to avoid gunfire—with real bullets!

C-rations were the only food available, delivered daily by personnel carriers. One day, in that cold October, our platoon missed lunch because our brass-polishing platoon leader was out to make extra points with the commanders. Now I was never one to enjoy going hungry, so I asked the sergeant if Stubs and I could go to the personnel carrier and bring back the grub for the platoon.

"We'll not eat until nightfall—and that's an order!" barked the sergeant. "In fact, you might not eat until morning."

As I walked away angry, I mumbled to Stubs, "He'll pay for this! Mark my words, he'll pay for this!"

My hard heart could carry a grudge for weeks, even months. Two weeks later, I was still plotting how to get even with the sergeant. Stubs was even getting a little worried about me. He hadn't seen this side of me before. Iceman was a dangerous man to cross.

This particular sergeant really bugged me. Most of the other officers relied on me for loans or dope or both, but this guy was so straight, he didn't seem natural. Not only was he straight, he was a real jerk to boot, as far as I was concerned.

The barracks were always cold at Wieldflichen; they hadn't been remodeled since World War II. They were heated only by cast-iron coal-burning stoves. Stubs and I shared a room down the hall from the hated sergeant.

"Rearick, take my coal bucket down to the bin and fill it up. On the double, Private!" Sergeant Arthurs bellowed one night.

I knew he was trying to needle me. He had been ever since maneuvers. He also knew about my drug-dealing and loan-sharking activities. A brainstorm came to me immediately. In our room I'd hidden a seven-inch CO_2 cartridge—the kind used to inflate military rafts—and it packed a real wallop.

"Yes, Sir!"

I reached under the bed, grasped the cartridge and shoved it down into our own coal bucket, making sure it was well hidden. I started down the hall to the sergeant's room.

"Iceman, you're crazy!" hissed Stubs. "It'll kill him, Man, I'm tellin' ya. It'll blow his head clear off! Don't do it, Iceman!"

Strolling into the sergeant's room with a big grin, I said casually, "Here, Sir, take mine for now. I'll fill yours and use it later in our stove."

Meekly I handed the coal bucket to Arthurs. As I'd concealed my hatred for him for days, he took the booby trap without suspicion.

Upon returning to our room, I motioned to Stubs and we hurried outside where it would be safer, stamping our feet to keep warm in the cold night air while waiting calmly for the explosion.

With deafening force, the CO_2 cartridge not only exploded, it also blew out the wall of what had been, moments before, Sergeant Arthurs's room. Soldiers ran in with fire hoses; everyone was yelling in the confusion. The medics arrived, and a large crowd gathered. Stubs

and I nonchalantly strolled to the cafeteria for a cup of coffee.

Amazingly, Sergeant Arthurs was not killed by the
blast. The only thing that saved him was that after he emptied our coal bucket into the stove, he went to his locker to
hang up his clothes. When the blast hit, the lucky sergeant
was behind the metal locker door. This alone saved his
life.

Shrapnel from the exploding stove had embedded itself
in the door, the mattress caught on fire and the entire
room incinerated. Sergeant Arthurs received second-
degree burns and was totally deaf for three months, but he
was still alive.

In the investigation that followed, Stubs and I were
hauled into court to testify. My testimony was: "Someone
musta planted that CO_2 cartridge in the coal bucket to kill
Stubs and me. If the sergeant hadn't ordered me to get
him some coal that night," I lied, "we would've been dead
ducks. We sure were lucky."

The jury bought my story. Sergeant Arthurs, on the
other hand, knew the real truth. So, from that time on, no
one hassled Iceman. But, like all utopias, paradise ended.

Without warning, in July 1965, I was suddenly thrown
into Mannheim Military Prison—literally a hell hole! It
was far rougher than any prison I'd been in in the States.
Twice, in three weeks, the entire prison erupted into
riots. Even on "calm" days I saw prisoners beaten or
stabbed to death, while weekly reports of suicide rumbled
throughout the prison. It was definitely not a place where
anyone could expect to survive for long—even Iceman.

Several days passed before I discovered why I was
there. The army was making a global crackdown on drug
use and they didn't want the extent of drug usage leaking

out to the press. Their investigation of the major dope problem in Germany had led them right to Pfc. Ronald David Rearick, who, by their reckoning, was one of the most notorious drug-dealing figures in the army at that time.

I wondered what they planned to do with me. I couldn't imagine who'd had the nerve to squeal on me. It probably didn't matter anyway because, at this rate, I'd probably be in Mannheim 'til my hundredth birthday.

To my pleasant surprise, I was in Mannheim only a month before they hauled me off to headquarters. I was handed a "208" Discharge (code number for Failure to Adjust). Having thoroughly investigated my nefarious activities, the army had decided it would be easier just to get rid of me rather than keep me in custody. That was probably so.

I had no idea what had become of Stubs; they had separated us when we were arrested. I reckoned that poor ole Stubs was probably still in Heinrich Himmler's cell, learning German.

By the end of 1965, I found myself back home in Salt Lake City.

10

Induction

How does a guy get hooked up with the Syndicate? It's probably different for every "soldier" who enters the ranks of the underworld. Well, my beginnings with The Family were anything but planned.

Back in Salt Lake the only job I could find was loading trucks for a freight company, but it beat a lot of other jobs around at the time. I liked the people there because they loved my old army stories, which sounded so outlandish that I didn't think most of them really believed I was that tough.

The great thing about this job was breaking in after hours and finding where everything was stored. There were always huge shipments of TVs, radios and typewriters—just waiting to be plucked. It took the company weeks to notice that an inventory unit was missing. By then, of course, it was too hard to trace it back to anyone.

I worked hard for one thing only: so I could get plenty of money to support my first love—the night life. Barmaids and hookers were my constant companions; I was really riding high.

It wasn't long, though, before I began thinking about Anna and little Kathy. Kathy would be about five now and I wondered how she was doing. But I knew it wouldn't be smart to try to see Kathy, because it had been so long since I'd had any contact with her or Anna and I'd been through so much. I figured it was probably best just to move on.

I began to spend more evenings with Mom now that she and Dad had divorced. The divorce was a move that we were all happy about. Mom had taken a lot of abuse from Smiley over the years, and she deserved better.

I realized my own marriage to Anna had been a wipe-out, but rationalized that it really wasn't my fault. I reasoned that Anna had been awfully immature and I didn't know much about being a dad to little Kathy. I was older now and thought it sure would be great to have a little woman around the house, one who didn't ask too many questions—especially when it looked like some real money-making opportunities would open up.

With that line of thinking, it wasn't long before wedding bells rang again—this time, in 1967 to Gwen. Gwen wasn't anything like Anna. She was brunette, while Anna was blond. Gwen was petite and shy; Anna was tall, lively and outspoken. Gwen was a real stay-at-home woman— just the kind I wanted. She also seemed to be somewhat afraid of me, which suited me just fine. Soon, Ron Jr. appeared in our lives.

* * * * * *

While Ron Jr. was still very young, my cousin Jack reappeared on the Salt Lake City scene. He was an Oakie like me and we'd been pals all the years we were growing up, but we made a frightening duo when together. The whole family cringed when we showed up at the same family event.

Jack was a pilot and owned his own Stinson plane. I was back peddling dope in the Salt Lake area and had quite a market going. With Jack's plane, we figured we could fly into Mexico ourselves and really make a haul, cutting out at least two or three middlemen, meaning more profit for us, of course.

This business venture appealed to Jack immensely, so in 1966 we began our "Tucson Game" drug runs into Mexico, across the Arizona border. Though we could load plenty of marijuana into the plane, pills seemed to be more cost-effective.

The underground labs in northern Mexico were just getting in full swing, so we could buy pills by the barrel with half a million in each. We then loaded them into the plane, quickly flew back across the border, and would have them out on Tucson's streets in a matter of days, at several hundred percent markup!

I decided we needed to expand our market by devising more ways to get the dope inland. About that time, one of my co-worker buddies (and best customers) was transferred to San Diego, so I approached him about getting in on some of the action. San Diego would make another great contact point for the barrels of pills from Mexico. In case it got too hot to land in Arizona, we could just fly on to San Diego, land there and have this buddy ship the barrels to Salt Lake, where I could pick them up at the freight company's loading dock when I was on shift.

Things were going great—at least for me. Gwen, however, was getting quite unhappy with our marriage. Also, I didn't seem to be able to handle little Ronny's crying any more than I'd been able to handle Kathy's. So I reasoned that Gwen was getting too lippy, that she wasn't the woman I'd married and that I was justified in spending my free time elsewhere.

My usual escape from something like this was to spend my free time at the Broken Wheel Bar, owned by a friend named Gary Rounder. Gary had played professional sports before buying the bar and he was an interesting fellow to be around. All the guys in the bar including myself liked to listen to his pro ball stories.

* * * * * *

I started doing some bouncing for Gary on Saturday nights, just for the fun of it. "Never miss a chance to fight" and "Get in and get it over quick" were my mottos. Everyone in the bar would chuckle when I blurted out these ideological phrases.

One night, some creep started hassling a well-dressed businessman sitting with a couple of younger men at a table close to me. The creep was about 6'4" and weighed about 240 pounds. He was a big, mean bruiser. I started getting bugged because this big dude kept picking on the old guy, who seemed to be in his late 50s with silver-gray hair. As far as I was concerned, the creep showed no class. The kicker came when the clumsy dude bumped into me and spilled his drink all over my suit. That's all I needed to get involved.

"Listen, Creep, the guy said to leave him alone and now you've dumped your dumn drink all over me besides. You just had to keep it up, didn't you? Now you've ruined my suit too. That does it!"

With that, he came at me. It got silent in the bar. Gary

88

came over with a broomstick. I didn't need it, so he just stood idly by and watched.

I let the dude swing at me like he was Rocky Marciano. Then I punched him hard, right in the Adam's apple. He crumpled, gasping for air. I followed with a swift kick to the groin, and the fight was over. He was carried out to his car and tossed on the front seat.

As the older gentleman left with the two young guys, he leaned over, patted me and said, "Thanks."

A week later, a call came from the gray-haired man, who turned out to be Vic Galli, the head of The Family, an organized crime syndicate whose territory covered all of Utah and Nevada. He had called Gary at the Broken Wheel to get my name and invite me over.

Vic greeted me in a mahogany-paneled office filled with antiques and Persian rugs. "I've checked you out, Mr. Rearick. Iceman, I believe it is. I'd like you to join my business."

Flattered by this and not one to give up acceptance by someone I admired, I quickly accepted his offer. I had a fairly good idea what his business was. Galli was the kingpin of the underworld operations in that area. All the way home, I kept glancing at myself in the rear-view mirror and saying, "Iceman, a member of The Family. Hey, Kid, you're hittin' the big time. No more small stuff. You're with Mr. Big now!"

I knew my life had just taken a new turn. Iceman was now in the real world of crime.

11

The Colombia Connection

I was really impressed with my new boss. I found myself looking in the mirror a lot more at home, because Vic's guys began teaching me how to dress, and introduced me to the "finer things in life": tailored suits, big cars and classy jewelry. I learned to tell real stones from phony ones. I also learned the difference between name brands and those of the common man.

A newcomer to The Family was never let in on the ground floor of any job, but this didn't bother me, as I expected to be "tested" for some time. At first, just being with these guys exhilarated me, and I knew Vic liked my style.

However, it did mean the end of my partnership with cousin Jack. If I was going to be one of Galli's men, Vic didn't want me hanging around any amateurs. It was hard for me to tell Jack it was over; but when you have a chance to move up in what you're good at, you do whatever it takes to get ahead.

About this time also, I decided I wasn't really a family man and Gwen thought it was best to part too. So, one evening, I kissed little Ronny good-bye for the last time, put some money in Gwen's hand and said, "See ya around, Babe."

I had reasoned that it was Gwen's fault our marriage didn't take. If she just hadn't kept putting so much pressure on me, I'd have been able to handle marriage a little easier. I didn't see why I should try so hard to work with Gwen when, being with these new friends of mine, I could have the pick of the bunch anyway. When women are so cheap, why should I bother with just one? After all, Vic's guys had some real ins.

This new job meant giving up my job at the freight company. It was about time anyway, as someone sooner or later was sure to trace those barrels of pills back to me. And I'd stolen enough stuff that I was sure some insurance investigator would eventually spot me if I didn't get out of it now.

Galli started me at a salary of $5,000 a week, with plenty of extra cash for "expenses"—like women and dope. At first, my job mainly entailed doing "special favors" for Vic, bill collecting, of sorts. Vic laughingly referred to me as his reminder notice. I loved my new job. Rearranging faces and busting up arms and legs was great fun for me, and Vic really liked my style.

My first assignment was to "remind" a secret gambling casino owner in Salt Lake that the Galli Family had been promised more of the action.

"Mr. Tecanzo lives alone," Vic informed me. "I don't want you to kill him; but once you find him, just *convince* him, because he's been talked to already. You know what I mean? I just want you to convince him."

I chuckled, "Convincing I understand. He'll be sure to understand. You can count on me, Mr. Galli."

I started off working with a kid named Joe, who had already been with The Family a couple of years and was related to one of Vic's closest confidants.

We found Tecanzo at his house and asked if he could come out back to talk. As he stepped outside the door, I slammed him on the back of his head and blood began to redden the back of his shirt. Joe grabbed his arm and twisted it to the right as far as he could while pulling it behind the man's back. Then I rubbed his nose hard enough on the pavement to draw blood, while Joe got a sledge hammer from the car. Holding Tecanzo's leg over the edge of the curb, I slammed the hammer down on his knee, breaking his kneecap. Silently and businesslike, we climbed into the car and left.

The next week, I was called to do a second job. This time, it was something Vic wanted to do to "help" a friend. Again, Joe was my partner. By now, I'd figured out that Joe went along so he could report on how I operated. I didn't mind because I was sure I could teach Joe a few things.

This time, we found our victim home asleep. We slipped in by a side window, bounded into his bedroom and threw on the lights. The poor guy thought he was going to be shot. He whimpered and begged for his life. I proceeded to pull the screaming, begging wimp out of bed and tossed him over to Joe. Joe threw the guy on the floor and held his arm out sideways while I took a flying leap and jumped onto the screaming man's arm.

The bone burst through the side of his arm; blood spattered on the wall and the bedspread. As we left I turned to the guy, writhing on the floor, and said icily, "Nice doin' business with ya."

With that, we strolled out to the car and drove off. All

the way back, we laughed about how this dude pleaded and begged for his life.

It wasn't long before Vic asked me to be his personal bodyguard. Whenever Vic had work to do, I went along. I was always paid in cash, and right on time, too.

Galli got me a job at a freight company shortly after I began spending a lot of visible time with him. Everyone who worked for The Family in Utah had to look as though they operated something legit. I would get a check mailed regularly to me, but all I really did was mess around with the forklift when I felt like it; or I simply said, "I have something to do," and would disappear for most of the day, to do my own thing. But for appearance sake it had to look as though I were a regular employee.

Vic was always careful, very careful. I learned immediately that you didn't mess with his instructions.

Within the year, I started making out-of-country flights with Galli. The drug trade was booming and the Galli Family was into it deep. It was on one of these trips that I learned it was actually some uncles of Vic's in New York who'd gotten him started in The Family. Vic's two younger brothers were part of the Utah-Nevada operation, as well.

I never did have much to do with his younger brothers. I just knew they existed when Vic would drop his guard and talk about The Family from time to time. I felt honored to be confided in about some of their secrets.

Usually my assignments came by a simple phone call. When Vic called me, he'd never say his name. He'd just say, "Pack your bags, Ron. We're goin' on a trip."

Then I would pack up, go by Vic's place and pick him up. We usually headed out for a lavish dinner, climbed aboard a Lear Jet and off we'd go. Nobody but Vic himself ever knew where we were headed.

The plane was always loaded with all the right weapons, and I was told to leave my .45 in the car. A usual type of operation would take us into a place like El Paso. Once we landed, we took a cab and met some people. Occasionally, we flew to New York, where we'd be picked up in a flashy car and whisked off to some meeting place. At other times, it would be Los Angeles. But most of the time, we flew to a small place outside Miami or to a shrimping town called Cameron, Louisiana.

Cameron was the place where, eventually, I would be responsible for meeting dope-laden boats from Colombia, South America. They'd load up a U-Haul truck and several vans and travel back caravan-style, leapfrogging across New Mexico and Utah. The last van was usually stuffed with furniture. A distance of several miles was maintained between vans, keeping constantly in touch via CB radios. About this time, I was promoted to Head of Operations for Galli.

Late in 1965, I got one of Vic's usual calls. I picked him up; we loaded into the Lear Jet, and off we went. When we'd been in the air for some time, I ventured to ask, "Where we headed tonight, Boss?"

Vic grinned. "South, my boy, where it all begins— Colombia, South America, the land of the big C."

There weren't too many people who knew about the origin of the cocaine trail in late 1965, and I was no exception. I was smart enough to figure out, however, that Galli was making a *big* transaction in Colombia, especially if he was going there in person.

"It sounds great!" was my response.

I'd always liked coke anyway. Maybe I'd get to try some of the Colombian stuff firsthand.

I felt the plane land as it glided in among the trees. It

was dark and kind of eerie dropping in at night into the middle of the jungle. The jet bounced to a stop and the lights around the airstrip vanished. Three jeeps sped up alongside the plane. The pilot and the other men were told to stay with the plane while Vic and I were invited to climb into the head jeep.

I could see that this was a professional operation, and noticed that the head man had an automatic rifle with an infrared scope attached. No one would escape these *bandidos* if they didn't want him to, that was for sure.

As we got into the jeep, all the Latinos in the other two jeeps kept their eyes glued on me. They all knew Vic wasn't going to cause a stir, but they were still wary of me. A few words were exchanged, and then off they sped. When we had gone a short distance from the plane, everyone seemed to relax.

I wanted to keep track of where we were going, so I kept checking my watch. We drove for about 25 minutes along well-kept jungle roads worn smooth by constant use. Finally, we came to an area surrounded by barbed wire. We passed through a gate guarded by four or five guards on each side, armed with poised machine guns.

The head man in the front jeep, with the infrared scope, said, "The fence marks the beginning of our wonderful mine fields. We're kept very safe in here, you see, very safe." We all laughed uncomfortably.

Then we drove for what I calculated to be about three miles from the barbed-wire fence to a warehouse. This was definitely a military operation. The warehouse was only one of many, with walls shaped like Quonset huts. Inside one of the huts we were shown where the cellophane was kept for wrapping the dope. Then we were led to another warehouse where the raw leaves were dried and stored. Finally, we were escorted to the refinery and the houses where it was all stored until it was sold.

I glanced around, trying to keep alert. I noticed several towers with manned machine guns pointed in our direction. The guide said, "They're men with machine guns. The lights can light up everything like daylight for about 300 yards, and those men never miss. But don't worry, they know you're friendly."

I was left at the lab, which wasn't like the labs in the States. This was more like a shack filled with the equipment of chemists. Men were processing drugs like madmen, seemingly oblivious to my presence.

I watched as Vic was loaded into a van and taken to a beautiful home on a hill overlooking the grounds. En route back to the States, Vic confided that it was the home of one Pedro Ricardo, who was a big businessman in Colombia with powerful political connections. His "family" had fleets of commercial jets to do "business" with. They flew their stuff into Canada, Miami and Europe—wherever and with how much anyone wanted of their "product."

As the Galli Family was making a big enough deal, Vic wanted to talk to Ricardo personally. Arrangements were then made. Everyone was introduced to me because, from this point on, I would be the contact man for Galli. I would connect with the lieutenants of the Ricardo Family, mostly from Cameron. There would be other trips to Colombia for me in the future.

On the second trip, I was allowed to come to the beautiful house on the hill, but was never allowed to meet Ricardo himself. I usually dealt only with the lieutenants of the operation.

On leaving the compound, we again pulled up to the barbed-wire fence. The guards tipped their hats and waved us on. This time, I enjoyed the trip through the jungle much more; it was interesting to listen to the different jungle sounds. Though I'd heard these sounds in movies, I never realized how realistically they'd been created.

I had guessed that Vic had made a pretty good deal, because everyone was so cheery as we drove back to the plane. Pointing to me, Vic said, "Mr. Rearick will be your contact in the future."

The head man, with the infrared scope in his rifle, then shook Vic's hand. "So glad to meet you. We look forward to many years of good business."

As we loaded the plane, the three jeeps of *bandidos* tipped their guns down and, turning, headed back into the jungle. As we lifted off the runway, we all heaved a great sigh of relief. We knew we'd ventured into very dangerous territory, but suspected it would make great payoffs for us. As the plane landed on the airstrip in Salt Lake, I was glad to be back home. Colombia was definitely in a league all its own.

* * * * * *

In January 1969, Joe and I made a standard trip into Mexico. This time, we traveled in a large motor home, complete with fishing rods for Baja, and other tourist props. We also carried a lot of cash to purchase a large order of dope.

When we arrived at the agreed-upon site, we found two strange kids waiting at the appointed time and place. An abandoned gas station on a lonely stretch of highway was our destination.

I became a little suspicious; I'd expected Juan and Julio, as prearranged. I didn't recognize the two guys who showed up. Both of them were young—only 20 or so—and sloppily dressed in grimy sweat-stained shirts. They were certainly not dressed in natty attire like the regular drug dealers. In addition, the battered station wagon they drove did not fit the picture of a drug ring car. Though their young faces looked tough, their unsteady steps revealed their nervousness.

"Julio couldn't make it today," said one. "But I'm his nephew."

Neither of the Mexican strangers carried packages that looked like they contained any drugs.

"Where's the stuff?" I asked.

"We want to see the payment first," came the reply from the other kid.

Joe and I glanced at each other, but stood silent and still. The Mexican kids could tell that their bluff was being called. Only 10 feet away, the kid on my right suddenly pulled out a gun and started firing.

"Get 'im!" Joe yelled, reaching for his revolver.

But my hand was quicker; my gun was already aimed. Simultaneously, I jumped to one side, pumping bullets into both Mexicans. We both leaped into the motor home and sped toward the border. I felt sick because I was sure I'd killed both of the kids—which honestly was not my intention. All the way back we tried to figure out how these two young Mexicans got wind of Julio's drug operation.

"Vic ain't gonna like this," Joe kept saying. "Vic's gonna be furious!"

"Shut up, Joe! Just shut up. I did what I had to do."

Vic was furious all right.

"But I had no choice," I bleated defensively as I faced Galli in his office two days later. "If *I* hadn't shot them, they'd have blown *us* away!"

"I know you didn't cause the incident, Iceman, but I still won't be sending you on any out-of-town jobs for a long time. You'll stay in Salt Lake and keep a low profile until this hassle dies down, because I'm tellin' ya, Iceman, those dudes don't forget. I have a lot invested in you, Iceman; you cost me plenty today."

One of the kids turned out to be the nephew of the kingpin for Galli's drug dealings in Mexico. Of course, the Mexican "godfather" was furious, even though—fortunately for me—his nephew lived. Galli figured that in time, though, the Mexican contact would cool down and eventually forget about the incident.

For months, I couldn't leave the Salt Lake area and felt like a kid who'd been grounded. All at once, there was no fun in this job anymore. I was sick and tired of all this stuff. *After all, hadn't I proved myself to Vic? You'd think Vic would side with me. Why don't we go bust that godfather down there in Mexico for not keeping his nephew in line? Why should I be punished? I've busted up people real good for Vic. I've stood with the dude and risked my neck in Colombia for him. It's not fair! I make one mistake and look what I get—thrown out in the cold.*

Over the months I complained. Sometimes I'd complain to Joe, but he wasn't one to enter into any complaints about Vic. Somehow, I figured when I got into the Syndicate I'd meet men with a higher code of ethics than the ordinary street fighters. Instead, I'd discovered that their code was "every man for himself." Instead of brilliance and cunning, I noted that the average Syndicate hoods often made stupid mistakes. But, more than that, I observed that the operation was filled with guys who were careless about what they said.

On the other hand, I wasn't one to let information

trickle out so that federal investigators, or the two Mexicans I'd cut down, could pick up on it. I decided then I wanted out.

First, I faced Galli, a little frightened. But Vic knew I hadn't been happy about returning to my job as his local muscle man, so he was ready for my announcement.

Straightforwardly, I said, "Hey, look, Mr. Galli, I gotta quit. I just can't handle it no more, being locked up in town. Besides, there's some other things I'd like to try out."

Galli had never had this sort of thing happen before. But to the surprise of everyone in his office, the big boss just nodded his head and grunted. Vic knew Iceman was tight-lipped and wouldn't go shooting his mouth off. He also knew I was more at odds with the law than most of his men, so he wasn't worried about my squealing about *his* operation. Besides, unknown to me, Galli had a lot on his mind. He was real close to being busted by the Feds and he knew it. Vic also figured that if I was an informant, I wouldn't have timed my quitting when I did.

* * * * * *

During my months of seclusion in Salt Lake, I had returned to Gwen and little Ronny, and we were trying to make our marriage work again—that is, when I wasn't partying all night or disappearing to do Galli's muscle work.

One night, without warning, Gwen confronted me, "Ron, when you leave here tonight, you might as well take all your clothes with you. I don't ever want you to come back. You left once and said you'd never come back, but you did. This time, Ronny and I don't ever want to see you again. Get outta here!"

Tears cascaded down her cheeks. *Maybe she really does love me, but just the same, I ain't gonna take that kinda talk from a woman and stick around. She doesn't know me at all if she thinks I'm gonna take that kinda stuff. Besides, if she did really know me, she probably wouldn't like me anyway. I'm no good. I've never amounted to anything.*

With these thoughts ringing in my mind, I packed my clothes, walked out and closed the door behind me without a word. I never went back.

The only other business I'd had any interest in at all was professional gambling and I had always dreamed of owning my own casino. From time to time I would imagine myself as a casino king—something like Humphrey Bogart had been in the movies I'd seen as a kid. In July 1971, I decided it was time to give it a shot and be my own boss.

Through my work for The Family I'd met a man named Harry Nugent, who had many years of experience operating casinos. In addition, Harry had potential blackmail information on the district attorney, so our underground operation would never be bothered. I decided it would be a good move.

I put up all the money for the gambling machines, and Harry and I became partners of Vegas North. I visualized hours of leisure and weeks of vacation in exotic spots—with Harry doing *my* bidding this time.

I really enjoyed this new venture for the first few months. I'd get all dressed up in formal attire and greet the guests. Yet, when it came time to start enjoying my leisure from the casino's profits, I realized there was none, because I constantly worried about Harry. I was sure

Nugent was taking money from the till when I wasn't looking. But as Nugent had the know-how and I had very limited business experience, I was on the hook, and locked in.

It didn't take long before I was fed up with the casino. One day, I told Nugent, "This casino's more of a ball-and-chain around my neck than marriage was. I want out. Harry, you give me $15,000 and the place is yours."

Harry was delighted. Within one day he handed me the $15,000. I took the cash and walked. As I drove away, I decided that what I needed was a vacation—a break from this stupid town. I needed to get clear out of Salt Lake and air out a little bit.

One of the customers I'd met during my casino venture was a cute gal named Rhonda, who had inherited a small fortune. When I left the casino, I looked her up and we began to live together. For several months I was a wealthy playboy.

Rhonda and I even flew out to Newport Beach on the California coast where we learned to sail. We made several trips to Acapulco for deep-sea fishing. Life was great. I decided this was the way life was meant to be lived. When we returned stateside, we spent most of that summer following the rock concerts around the West Coast. We stayed high on psychedelics, coke and heroin, while we listened to some of the great rock stars of that time.

Eventually, we found our way back to Salt Lake City. One night that summer, during a coke and heroin party, a near tragedy happened.

Suddenly, a gal screamed, "Eddy! Eddy! Oh, No! He's overdosed! He's gone!"

I pushed the hysterical girl aside and picked up Eddy's limp, clammy body. I dumped him into the tub and filled it with water. Then I got a lamp from the bedroom, plugged it in near the tub and threw it into the water.

Sparks flew! The lamp exploded! Eddy's limp body convulsed with the force of the electric shock. An instant later, I pulled out the plug. Though poor Eddy lay there as stiff as a board, he was at least breathing.

I had learned this trick over the years and had seen a number of dopers shocked back to life this way. Usually they were propped up in a shower and didn't get as much of a jolt as Eddy had in the filled tub. But this apartment didn't have a shower, so I had to act fast if I were going to save his life. I was just glad the kid lived. I told the others to keep Eddy warm and awake by walking him around and feeding him coffee until he could function on his own again.

When I went into the bedroom to calm down, I found a tiny two-year-old lying on the bed sucking on a bottle. When she heard me come in, she turned glazed eyes toward me and tried to stand up, but couldn't. The poor little thing was drunk!

I knew her folks had put wine in her bottle—maybe even drugs—to keep her subdued while they partied. The combined incidents of dealing with Eddy's OD and seeing the pathetic little girl made me sick.

"That's it! This is all insane! Only crazy people live like this! I've had it with this kind of life!"

I stalked out and slammed the door. The next day, I found myself in Rhonda's mountain cabin, trying to think things through. Those feelings were gnawing at me again. I just couldn't stand to see people taken advantage of. Whether it was a little two-year-old girl on wine or some kid on smack, I just couldn't handle it anymore.

However, my hardened heart didn't know how to handle the tension that was produced by this sensitivity. I just knew there was more to life than this.

I'd gone through a lot that year. The Syndicate hadn't worked out for me, I'd failed at being a casino king and the playboy life had been a washout. Maybe suicide was the way out. There had to be some end to it all, or I knew I'd find myself at a crazy farm.

Several days later, I returned to Salt Lake, but only long enough to shower, pack my clothes and take off for Las Vegas. I decided to relax and gamble until I came up with a plan, a plan that would change the course of my life forever.

Most of my money had been gambled away by the time I ran into a connection I'd known while with The Family. He offered to fix me up with some coke.

I dealt out a few drugs around town, gambled away my take, partied, got another load of drugs, dealt them out, gambled some more and partied all over again. And so it went. It was one big cycle.

It was then I encountered the kid who pulled a gun on me, and that's when the plan to heist the million dollars from United Airlines came to light—the plan that seemed now to have gone awry.

12

Arrest and Conviction

I called my attorney, Phil Harris, to announce that I'd been arrested that afternoon with a million bucks on the front seat of my car.

He just chuckled and asked, "Rearick, what am I gonna have to get you out of next? Hang tough and I'll check into it."

Then they marched me off to my cell. The way I figured it, I was probably okay; but, just in case, I'd better start accepting that I'd be in jail awhile. I always hated county time in jail. As far as I was concerned, it was the hardest time to serve. But at least the jail in Salt Lake City was better than the average. I also decided I should get "comfortable," as I saw no reason to suffer while I was kept in this hole.

The first business I needed to take care of was to find a guard I could bribe. I knew I'd have to bide my time because it would be much too risky to offer a guard money right off. So I watched to see which guards were interested in porn. I'd learned this trick some time back from guys in the underworld: If you catch a guy who's interested in porn, you can get your "claws" into him real easy and get just about anything you need thereafter.

One day, during visiting hours, one of my buddies came to see me. Instructing my buddy to put his ear close to the visiting booth screen, I whispered, "Hey, Man, send me up a gal. You know, one of the gals you've got, one of the young ones. Send her up to see me and I'll tell her what I want done after she gets here."

I knew my buddy would accommodate me because a lot of people owed me in a big way, including him.

The next day, a cute 17-year-old hooker appeared at the jail to see "Ronny." I had been covertly watching one of the guards on this shift and noticed that he'd been eyeing some of the gals visiting other prisoners. In addition, this guard's constant companion was a *Playboy* magazine.

Calling the guard over, I said, "Hey, Pal, let me introduce you to Sally. Sally, this is Bill."

"Nice to meet you," Bill responded. "Rearick, what do you want with a nice gal like this?" Turning to Sally, Bill asked, "What's a lady like you doin' up here?"

"Bill, how would you like to get to know Sally, I mean real well? You know what I mean? Sally says she thinks you're cute and really likes you."

The hook was set. The guard bought the bait. So, in exchange for turning his head when my scotch and dope arrived during his shift, I arranged it so Bill could meet Sally privately a couple of times a week.

From then on, Salt Lake City Jail was like my personal penthouse. Mom brought me plenty of fried chicken and lots of fruit, and my good buddy brought me scotch and a few joints stashed in a lunch basket whenever he came to see me.

My attorneys, Phil Harris and Robert Van Haven,

were both certain the Feds had no case against me.

Phil assured me, "Look, Ron, you've got a bad record, but they can't bring your past into this case. It's not your voice on the tape you sent to the airlines, and the tape's their only evidence. We've also got an expert witness who'll testify that the voice is not yours. So you had a million bucks in the car with you, so what? Your story still makes sense. And, finally, there aren't any witnesses. I'm tellin' you, Ron, they don't have a case against you."

Van Haven added, "You're going to walk, Ron. You'll be home free."

On April 15, 1972, the trial began in the Superior Court of Salt Lake City: The State of Utah and United Airlines vs. Ronald David Rearick, a/k/a Iceman. The charges: "Interfering with commerce by threats of violence, conveying information to destroy an airliner and its passengers and attempted extortion against United Airlines."

The questions that worried me and kept bugging me during the case were: What happened to my pistol? If the Feds ever found that weapon, I knew I was a goner for sure. And what about the Browning automatic rifle? As far as I knew, it was probably rusting in the desert somewhere. And what about Stubs? What happened to him? Did he also get caught, and squeal?

When one of the state's prosecutors entered the tape into evidence with Stubs's voice demanding the million dollars from United Airlines, he insisted that it was my voice on the tape. Contrary to the assurance of my lawyers, the voice expert couldn't prove or disprove that the voice on the tape was mine.

In addition, the jury had been informed that the money recovered had been found in my possession. Add to that the fact that I didn't have a solid alibi and that my past record *was* introduced into evidence, over the objections of my attorneys, you can guess the outcome.

At times, the trial scene was almost comical. Judge Willis Ritter, known as the hanging judge, was truly a fearsome person to stand before. No one dared cross him! The prosecutors, the defense attorneys all walked on eggshells in his courtroom.

During one of the afternoon sessions, street workers were breaking up the sidewalk on the street below with an air compressor, making a lot of racket. It was very difficult for the judge to hear. So he stopped the proceedings and had the court clerk go tell the workers to halt their work until court adjourned. Timidly, the clerk left the courtroom, reappearing a few minutes later, but below the jackhammer could still be heard.

"Clerk, I thought I told you to have those men stop that hammering down there," demanded Judge Ritter.

"I did tell them, Your Honor. But they said they couldn't stop, unless their boss gave them the order," replied the clerk.

"Very well, then. Get some assistance and arrest those street workers for contempt of court! Bring all their equipment with them and they can just sit here until I can get to their case. Have you got that?"

"Yes, Your Honor."

"Good! Then see to it."

Within a few minutes, the clerk returned with the crew of four men in tow, while a policeman carried their jackhammer and compressor hoses. The crew was directed to a bench at the back of the courtroom. Though everyone was in utter dismay, no one dared cross the judge.

The trial had been in session again only a few minutes

when the work crew's supervisor strode angrily into the courtroom.

"Judge, what're you doin' with my crew?" he demanded.

"Your crew happens to be in contempt of court, Sir. Would you like to post their bail?"

"What kinda jerk are you? You can't stop a city work crew, just so you can have a quiet court! Who do you think you are, anyway?"

"You're going to find out who I am, right now! I'm charging *you* with contempt of court also. You can all post bail and we'll set a trial date."

Meekly, they posted bail, and their equipment was wheeled back out of the courtroom. I never did hear the outcome of this case, but for the remaining time my trial was in progress, the jackhammer remained silent on the street below.

After three days of deliberation, the jury found me "guilty as charged." On May 10, 1972, I was returned to the courtroom for sentencing. I figured I was in deep trouble—particularly when I remembered how unkind and irascible the judge had been to the street work crew a few weeks before. If Judge Ritter was that harsh and unfair to a work crew who hadn't done anything unlawful, just think what he'd do to someone like me.

The morning of sentencing I was very alert. My eyes darted around the courtroom searching for a chance to escape. Of course, that was impossible since both my hands and feet were shackled. Desperation welled up within me.

My attorney leaned over. "He's going to go hard on you, Iceman. They've been after you for years. I did all I could, Iceman, I really did. I can't believe they found you guilty. I thought we had a pretty good case."

It had already been decided by my attorneys that an appeal would be of little value, so they were going to let the law take its course. The courtroom was packed; I was only one of three hijackers to be sentenced that day. I wondered again, What happened to Stubs?

Mom was there, tears brimming in her eyes. My sister Sue and her current husband were there, too. On the presiding bench sat the same "hanging judge"—72-year-old Willis Ritter—the same harsh man who had presided at my trial the month before. Judge Ritter had earned this nickname because he meted out extremely harsh sentences and he rarely recommended parole.

The first prisoner called to the bench for sentencing was Earl Coleman, who appeared to be mentally imbalanced. He had hijacked a jet out of Dallas with only a water pistol and pocketknife. Needless to say, he had been captured the minute the jet landed in Utah. Judge Ritter looked up, fixed a steely gaze on the hapless man, smiled big and then began.

"Earl Coleman, this court has found you guilty of extortion. You are hereby sentenced to 15 years in the federal penitentiary at Springfield, Missouri. Do you have anything to say to this court?"

Coleman just shrugged his shoulders and stared off into space.

"Very well. You may take the prisoner away," the judge ordered.

The next prisoner was more of a live wire. His name was John McCoy, a veteran of the Vietnam War. He had returned from war filled with hatred and vengeance, nursing an explosive temper—a temper so uncontrolled, I heard, that one night his folks, out of fear for their own

110

lives, had to call the police to their home.

It seems that McCoy had masterminded a half-million-dollar hijacking scheme against Pacific Southwest Airlines. He had planned to bail out of the plane somewhere over Provo, Utah, with all the money in hand—just like D.B. Cooper had. His plan backfired. His folks turned him in. Judge Ritter began again.

"John McCoy, this court has found you guilty of extortion and of holding passengers for ransom. You are hereby sentenced to 45 years in the federal penitentiary at Leavenworth, Kansas. Do you have anything you want to say to this court?"

With a sneer, McCoy turned towards the courtroom onlookers. "Yeah, I do. The first thing I'm goin' to do when I get out is kill my folks and my brother." He pointed a menacing finger at them.

The onlookers gasped. McCoy's family shrank back, obviously terrified. I could have killed McCoy for saying that! The last thing I needed was to have this tough old judge all riled up, just before sentencing me.

Slamming his gavel angrily on the desk, Judge Ritter blazed, "Get that man out of here, right now!"

Later, I learned that only six months later Coleman had hanged himself with a bedsheet. As for McCoy, he had managed to break out of prison with another hardened con and was killed a year later in a shoot-out with Chicago police.

I ground my teeth. A nervous twitch started in my left eye. Just gazing at Judge Ritter made my stomach turn. I could see that the judge was really stirred up. It looked bad for me. As I clanked up to the bench, shackles dragging, I thought, "But I wasn't even armed when they caught me. I didn't hold any hostages, like McCoy did. I didn't hurt anybody, and they even got their million bucks back."

"Ronald Rearick, approach the bench," ordered the judge.

I stepped forward a couple of feet. Everyone in the courtroom was quiet. I could hear Mom crying softly. Sue and her husband were trying to comfort her.

"Ronald Rearick, this court has found you guilty, as charged, of violating the *U.S. Penal Code*, Section 18. Will the court clerk read us this man's record."

The clerk began to read, and read, and read. I didn't think she'd ever stop reading. Iceman's list of criminal offenses included 14 jail terms and two prison terms. I'd even forgotten some of the offenses until they were read off. Most of the crimes I'd committed for The Family weren't even on the list.

Balefully, I glared up at the judge when the monotone voice finally finished reading. Judge Ritter was smiling— and that was never a good sign where Judge Ritter was concerned. I had heard that the "hanging judge" always smiled just before he pronounced a particularly stiff sentence. My heart sank.

"Mr. Rearick, you are hereby sentenced to 25 years in the McNeil Island Penitentiary. Do you have anything to say to the court today?"

Without even thinking, I stupidly blurted out, "Yeah, I have just one thing to say, Judge. I'm goin' to kill ya when I get out! You're a dead man, Judge. You're a dead man!"

Behind me, my family gasped in disbelief. As they hustled me out of the courtroom, I glanced over at my attorney. He just shook his head and said, "Ron, you didn't help yourself. You blew it. You didn't help yourself one bit."

I could hear the chains echoing down the hall as I was

escorted to a holding cell, where I would be kept until the Feds took me to McNeil Island. That night, as I tried to sleep, I kept hearing two sentences from the past. One was what Pop had said so often: "You're *no* good, Ronald Rearick . . . you're *never* going to amount to anything!"

The other was from the elderly grocer, who had stood holding his wife's trembling hands while I robbed them of $70. "Son, God has something better for you."

These two statements kept bouncing around in my head, but Pop's words were stronger. Perhaps Pop's words were coming true after all.

13

McNeil Island

A federal prisoner is always transferred with great care from county jail to the federal prison. Precautions are taken to ensure against any chance of escape. My reputation had preceded me. The Feds knew I had a lot of buddies around Salt Lake City who would be willing to lend me a hand, so they weren't taking any chances.

The *last* night in a county jail is always the best. At least, in the joint (federal prison), I knew I would get to walk around. There wouldn't be so many drunks hanging around either; and all those punks, who didn't know anything about life, wouldn't be there to bug me.

I knew how to get my mind ready for prison life. The day I returned from my sentencing, the other felons were silent. They glanced up for only a moment to look at my face, then returned to rolling their cigarettes and playing cards. No one said a word to me. One young kid, who I'd started calling Popeye, came over and tried to comfort me. I slammed him up against the bars and snarled, "Leave me alone or I'll kill ya!"

After all, I was about to enter a different world with a

whole new set of rules, a world where terror and muscle were the only securities a man had. I figured I had to start acting tough and getting psyched up or I'd never survive McNeil Island.

The next morning I got up in the holding cell and turned in my coveralls. I was handed a pair of denim jeans and a shirt, with I.D. numbers on the inside band of the jeans and the collar. I knew these would be traded in also, once I got to McNeil.

The Feds are always a little more careful than the county fuzz. It was kind of humorous to watch them look down on the county yokels. I winked at the guard to whom I'd introduced the young chick. "Thanks for making my stay so *comfortable.*" The Feds prepared to shackle me.

As the guard knelt down to shackle me, the chains jangled. The Fed guard nodded as he asked, "Rearick?"

"Yup, that's me, and I'm ready for my getaway."

I laughed. He didn't.

The afternoon Utah heat was unbearable in the cells, but as soon as the guards opened the door and stepped in, I could feel the nice, cool breeze from the air conditioner over the officers' desks. Small coolers in the windows made it slightly more bearable in the jail's outer section of the holding cells.

First, my hands were chained together. Then another chain was wrapped around my waist and locked to my hands, limiting my reach to about four inches from my body. Next, they shackled my feet with about a foot of chain between so I could walk. Finally, a single chain was run from my feet and connected to my hand chains. They were making quite certain I wasn't going anywhere. Even if I tried, I wouldn't be moving too fast.

"You guys got this down to an art, ain't cha?" I commented as I leaned back, smoked a Camel and watched the smoke rings disappear through the cell's ventilation system.

"Okay, Rearick, get up! Let's hit the road, you guys. We've got a few hours ahead of us before nighttime," barked the Fed guard to the county fuzz and me.

As we drove across the plains around the city, I thought it would probably be the last time I'd get to see the Salt Lake horizon. After a three-day, cross-country trip, chained hand and foot in the patrol car, I awakened one afternoon to catch my first glimpse of the greenish-blue waters of Puget Sound in Washington State.

I'd heard a lot about McNeil Island. I knew some of the roughest, toughest cons in the country would be there. At the ferry landing, I could see the prison above the trees. I knew a whole new life—not necessarily a good one—awaited me. This time, however, with a 25-year sentence hanging over me and a label of "an habitual criminal" by Judge Ritter, it didn't seem likely that I'd ever come out—alive.

It was about a two-mile trip to those dismal-looking, foreboding and intimidating walls. The ferry ride across the Sound was beautiful, however. As I looked forlornly at the high, gray walls on the eastern edge of McNeil Island, I mused as to whether I'd meet anyone inside I knew. I guessed there'd probably be some "quality" guys in there—guys with good reputations—the kind that were in for white-collar crimes, like extortion and income tax evasion.

One of the prisoners riding with us was a first-timer. We picked him up in some podunk town in Oregon. He was either crying or cussing at the guards. We called him The Fish. It'd only be a couple of days before The Fish would be turned into someone's drag queen. I planned to stay away from him, once I was inside.

The thoughts uppermost in a man's mind on his way to prison are: how to prepare himself—psyche himself up—to survive inside the pen and how to be "comfortable" while there. Getting comfortable is of primary concern. The lifers usually have this down to a science.

A first-timer in the joint prefers to be checked into isolation until his mind catches up with him and he gets his emotions sorted out. The dazed look of a newcomer speaks volumes in the pen: It's like an open, bleeding wound in a shark pond.

The car rolled off the ferry and drove up to the first gate. Papers were peered at and then cleared by the men checking vehicle authorizations. They poked inside the car to make certain they had the right prisoners. Then the car moved on inside the gates. We drove right up to the front of the medium-sized administration building, where we were marched inside the gate. Several other cons were being admitted at the same time. We were all searched and told to shower. Then we were ordered to don white coveralls, which would distinguish us from the rest of the prisoners. They gave us prison slippers that are invariably too small or too big.

I was strip checked first. The prison doctor poked and prodded me everywhere he could. The guard had me bend over for the drug check. My teeth were checked. By now, there were four of us being indoctrinated.

I'd already begun to scope out the guards for any weak ones. One of the inductees seemed very comfortable with what was coming down. I figured him to be at least a three-time loser.

Then we were escorted to the duty lieutenant. He

117

read off to us the list of rules. None of us really listened to the twerp. "Okay, you guys have a month to find a bunk. You can sleep in the isolation unit for the first month. After that, unless you check yourself into isolation, you'll be assigned to a cell."

The lieutenant droned on. "You've all been given a list of available jobs. Fill out the applications and get them into my box in the administration wing within a few days."

"Any infraction of the rules—fighting, perversity, ragging on the guards, or illegal contraband—entitles you to one week in the "hole" (solitaire). There you get fed once a day—usually old food made very cold just for you. There's no toilet or toilet paper, just a sleeping mat and a bucket."

"A second infraction of the rules gets you 30 days; a third infraction gets you 60 days. And, by then, you won't have a mind left for us to worry about."

He paused and grinned.

"You're here because you're federal criminals, a threat to society and unfit to be free. Hopefully, your experience at McNeil will return you to society as somebody useful and respectable."

We all laughed a short, self-conscious laugh. It hurt to hear these things, though none of us would admit it. It seemed as though we'd just stepped down one notch below being a full-fledged human. I could hear Pop's mocking voice again, saying he *knew* I'd never amount to anything. It sure looked as though it was now being proven.

Turning to the guards, the lieutenant barked, "Okay, guards, these men are ready for their isolation cells."

It felt great to be able to walk without the shackles, but for several days I could still hear them clanging in my ears. That first night I slept lightly because the poor slob from

Oregon cried most of the night. I knew he was a goner. I decided to bet on how long it would take before he got raped.

"Hey, Larry," I chimed out from the dark (the name of the other veteran con inducted with me) "whatcha give this guy? One or two days before he gets raped?"

"Oh hell, I'd say three or four hours," Larry responded with his husky voice that had the ring of an experienced con. We both laughed as I lit up a cigarette that sent a tiny flash of light through the cell block. The Oregon punk cried some more and we finally all dropped off into our separate, fitful sleeps.

Larry won the bet. Within two days the Oregon guy signed himself into protective custody. Though he didn't dare say why, we all knew he'd been marked as someone's "queen."

I checked out of the fish tank (isolation unit) after five days. A first-timer usually stays in the fish tank for up to two months, even though you're told at induction that you can stay only a month. Usually, however, you can stay for two, especially if you're showing signs of prison shock. I, on the other hand, was anxious to get out of there and pick my cell.

Now, at first, cell-choosing is up to the inmate. But if you don't find one soon enough, you're assigned one. An assigned cell was usually dangerous, because you would most likely be put in with some nut or a bunch of snitches, which would be life-threatening to everyone in that cell. Once, I'd seen a snitch ignited in his cell and burned alive! So I'd learned from that gut-wrenching experience to be very careful about choosing a cellmate. A smart con tries to find a cell with someone in it he knows. If that's not possible, he looks around until he finds what looks like a clean, quiet cell and then he kicks some guy out.

A hardened con, a professional inmate, was always easy to spot. Real cons keep their "house" tidy. They usually have an extra chair and nicer blankets. At the time, there were approximately 3,700 inmates, which made for quite a collection of rooming opportunities.

The fourth day out, when I was on the grounds during free time, I found a guy I knew from Utah, named Jess, who said there was an extra bunk in his cell. When I checked in, I found that, besides Jess, there were six other guys. That would make eight of us sharing a $12' \times 12'$ room. Definitely a little crowded for eight burly men.

Two sets of bunk beds stood end-to-end against each wall. Between the beds stood a battered table. Opposite the barred entrance to the cell was a three-foot-high bookcase, with the sink and toilet behind it. Under each bunk were footlockers for our underwear and a few belongings.

Jess introduced me to each of the guys. One guy, called John, was lying, half-awake, on one of the lower bunks, with an empty bunk above him. Now, I've never really liked sleeping on a top bunk, and I knew I needed to establish myself as one not to mess with, so as I climbed up to the bunk, I purposely stepped on John's face and ground my foot into it—hard. Pretending an apology, I said, "Oops!" That night I ended up in the lower bunk.

It wasn't much, but I knew it was to be my new home for many years to come.

Like any penitentiary, McNeil Island contained a wide range of criminals. Two of the guys in my cell were doing 75 years. Another had a 90-year term. And still another claimed a 300-year sentence! I didn't really believe that last one until Jess confirmed it. I'd heard of that kind of sentencing, but had never really met anybody in any of the state joints with such "honors."

As I walked around the yard talking to guys, I met men who were serving as much as 600-year sentences! Many of the trusties, the model prisoners, I met had been in prison since the 1930s. I even ran into foreigners convicted as spies and an Eskimo serving time for cannibalism! It sent chills up and down my spine, just thinking about the kind of guys I was living with.

The yard at McNeil Island was approximately 200 yards in length. So, with 3,700 prisoners, it wasn't exactly spacious. I spent the first few weeks just surveying the place and deciding how to get in on any of the action around.

I was assigned to be a hospital cook for those prisoners on special diets. This was the kind of job you wanted to latch onto if you could, 'cause you could get a steak now and then. Not only did it mean you ate better than the rest of the guys, but you'd be able to trade a little food for drugs or cigarettes.

Cigarettes are the usual currency in penitentiary living. Cartons of cigarettes and rations flowed like $20 and $100 bills.

Getting comfortable wasn't any real problem for me. By working in the hospital, I was easily able to rip off a needle and some pills. It wasn't at all tough to score. In fact, I was surprised at how easily hash and pot were available. It was good stuff, too—at least as good as any I'd ever smoked on the street.

I watched this medical trusty, a Jewish guy named Freddy, who was working in the hospital with me. He had been a medic in the Korean War. It was obvious he was stealing pills and selling them to the prisoners.

One day, when I caught him slipping some pills off a counter, Freddy graciously offered to let me in on the profits. I stifled a laugh, pretending to be honored and acting as though I'd had nothing to do with the drug trade. Another afternoon, when I happened to be standing behind a door, I caught Freddy tipping a chair over, prying a rubber tip off the end of the leg, and inserting a wad of bills in the hollow, metal tube.

The next day, I decided to dip into Freddy's money supply—just like the old days when I helped myself to the till in the saloon. It was a simple matter to search the chair legs in the room. I made off with $400 in cash and 30 "uppers." Then I cut slits in a thick newspaper, inserted the pills, taped the bills in and folded the paper so that even if it were unrolled, it would look normal. These kinds of precautions were important; anytime I was on my way back to my cell—especially from places like the hospital—I could be randomly searched.

I took the $400 and a guard I'd blackmailed purchased a pound of marijuana from outside. We got money, booze and drugs into the joint several ways. One way was to buy off a guard. This particular guard had been bought off.

It's easy to spot a guard who can be bought off. He's usually the one who's complaining. If you find a guard who is griping constantly about his boss or the job, who looks a little down, you just work on him. It takes six to eight guys sometimes, but we had it down to a science.

One day, one of us would walk up to a guard and comment on how good we ate in the joint, and wasn't it too bad he probably didn't eat that well at home, especially as we were both in prison, so to speak. Some of my favorite lines were: "You know, Pal, when I get sick here, I get the best doctors. In fact, they bring in the best Navy doctors to help me when I'm sick—and I'm a criminal. What do they give you when your kids get sick? Oh, they give you a little bit of insurance. But, really, you're no better off than I am. I'll bet they don't pay you much, either."

It takes only a few months before you can spot a guard who will buy dope for you. On the outside, we'd get one of our buddies to meet the guard and give him $5,000 to bring in a large stash. Photos were taken, the drugs were exchanged and another appointment would be made. On the second visit, the photo of the guard handling the money and drugs was presented to him. From then on, the guard was happy to do it for free.

On this particular occasion, we took the pot and broke it down for sale. We were able to double our money, and there was plenty of pot left for us. From then on, I was in business.

The best way to make money in the pen was with heroin and coke, even though in 1972 psychedelics were also moving freely at McNeil. However, coke and heroin made prison life generally much more bearable. One of our favorite pastimes was dropping some powerful hits of orange sunshine acid (LSD) and playing pinochle. Wow! Could that ever scramble a guy's brains.

As professionals, we had a number of ways to get drugs into the "big house." I looked around and found the young punk from Oregon. By now, the poor slob had been pretty well brutalized by some of the cons. So we took him up to the third floor and asked him if he'd like to help us bring in some coke and heroin. If he would, we wouldn't throw him over the railing. If he wouldn't, he could bet on being a dead man. Of course, he was "happy" to help us out.

Usually, I liked to find a guy who had had no drug

record on the outside and who came from a clean family. Then we'd "convince" him to bring drug deliveries. The kid from Oregon fit these requirements.

One of the guys a few cells down from us worked in the records room, so he got us a list of several cons who would work out well. We had him enter a gal's name on the kid's record as being passed for visitation rights. To prepare a delivery, she placed thumbnail-sized amounts of cocaine or heroin inside a deflated balloon, and secured it with a knot. She then held several of these in her mouth and passed them on to the kid when she kissed him. After he returned to his cell, he walked across the grounds to the dispensary to pick up a large dose of laxative. When the guy had a bowel movement, the balloons were removed and their contents passed on to us.

Several of us would cut the drugs down and distribute them in the exercise yard to other cons. It was a lucrative business, indeed. Within the year, I was able to buy whatever I needed in the pen. My buddies and I enjoyed a constant supply of steaks and whatever else we wanted.

We purchased steaks by two methods: we either traded some smack (heroin) or simply used threats. Other times, a little hash would do the trick. A guy working in one of the cooking areas would pass the meat along through several janitors or trusties. *No one* messed with a delivery to me.

When the meat arrived through our "delivery" system, we sliced it up, put it inside some coffee jars and ran hot water on them in our sink. The water was so hot, it literally boiled the meat. A few smokes, some joints, a couple lines of coke, our strips of steak and a good game of pinochle—life was great—limited, but great!

Drugs kept most of us comfortable; they kept us from

going insane. The more comfortable I could keep my buyers, the more comfortable life was for me. However, though we'd found a guard we could buy off, our troubles weren't over. Regular, random searches made it tough to carry on our enterprise. Finally, we connected with Joe, a guy serving several centuries of time. Joe worked in the warden's office.

By this time, the mid-1970s, detective dogs were being used to sniff out drugs and had become a common part of prison life. That added to the worries we had whether other cons would find our stash. One of the great games the prison racial gangs played was stealing each other's drugs.

Many prison riots are actually caused by the interruption of the flow of drugs, or by the monopolization of the drug trade by one gang over another. We made it a point to avoid any connection with any of the race gangs in the big house. Ours was strictly an enterprise, strictly professional cons getting comfortable.

Through Joe we were able to come up with an ingenious plan to store the drugs. It came to us one night during one of our pinochle games when we were all stoned on LSD. We devised a plan to have Joe hide our stash in the warden's office.

It also happened to be the night when the fuzz decided to have a check search of several cells on our block. And ours was first.

We had hidden our scotch whiskey in our coffee jars, had smuggled the steak into the cell and were all playing pinochle. When the cops busted in, we were all zooming on LSD, hallucinating, not even able to speak. Our mouths were like cotton. They searched our cell thoroughly, but, amazingly enough, didn't check the coffee jars. They never found the booze, so they simply assumed that we were all just acting crazy. One guy stood by the wall talking to himself, frightened out of his wits because of the surprise check. A couple of us walked him around, pretending that he'd just awakened and was a little fuzzy.

Though the fuzz were suspicious, no one in the joint gets too aggressive about trying to stop the flow of drugs. Any inmate or prison cop knows that it's the drug flow that keeps things calm in an overcrowded penal system.

When we all returned to our cells, we got paranoid. (LSD is known to cause extreme paranoia.) So we devised a plan that had us all down on the floor.

We decided we wouldn't stash our dope in the exercise yard anymore where it was subject to theft, nor would we stash it in our cell. Then it hit me like a bolt of lightning. "Why don't we get Joe to not only adjust the records, but also to stash our dope in the warden's office? The dogs will never sniff it out. They'll never suspect it because it wouldn't even occur to them to look there. How 'bout that for a great plan, huh?"

Joe was contacted and "convinced" to help us. The plan was a gem. He would enter the warden's office, pop the rubber caps off the bottoms of the chair legs, and stuff our coke, LSD and heroin up into them. When an order came in, we simply gave the "prescription" to Joe. While cleaning, Joe removed the drugs from the chair legs; then we delivered them the next day. We even had him stash our money in the chair legs, right under the warden's nose.

Moves like this made prison life a delight at times. We could laugh at night, even though the moans and cries of other inmates could be heard up and down the cell blocks. Beating the system made prison life tolerable. When I saw young men thrown off third- and fourth-tier levels to the concrete floor below, their skulls crushed by the force of the fall and their brains oozing out, it was a relief to be able to chuckle about the warden's own chair being the hiding place for our stash.

Having once again baffled the system brought us all to life again. It gave us that sense of superhuman existence in a fantasy world we were able to create in our minds, in direct contrast to the horrible life we lived that was like hell itself around us. It helped to buffer the animallike nature of man he exhibits when locked up for any length of time.

We got through many a night just being able to laugh about the warden sitting on a stash of drugs—and not even knowing it!

14

The Slow Meltdown

I spent most of my time at the iron pile lifting weights. There, I could handle most of my drug transactions after my work duties at the hospital. At one point though I nearly lost my job. When one of my delinquent customers happened to come into the hospital for treatment, I worked him over in the middle of the night, reminding him that he needed to make his bills good, even in the joint. Everyone had a pretty good idea who did the facial arranging on the guy, but he didn't talk, and neither did I.

It was 1973. Things were becoming a little uncontrollable in the joint. One day one of the guys in our cell we called Kid started cracking up. He just began hollering, "I can't take it any more. I can't take any more time. You guys have got to kill me. I'm too chicken to do it myself."

I had seen this kind of strange action in prison before. It was a bad sign. It was a moment that called for tenderness, but we all acted true to the character of all the men in there. Instantly, we all hardened. We knew that any show of weakness, like kindness, would mean certain death in our world. So we all laughed and began to mock the poor guy.

"Aw, come on, Kid. You've only got 99 years to go. What are ya worryin' about? Hey, they know about the drugs. They'll probably find them tonight, and you'll get another couple hundred years anyway."

Of course, this didn't help. He started yelling and hollering again. We were all a little bugged by his outburst. We didn't want to draw any attention to our cell so three of us agreed to help him kill himself.

One guy leaned over and asked, "Hey, Man, how do you want to go? You want to be choked? You want to be sliced? What do you want? You want to go off the tier head first?"

Kid replied, "Slice me. Slice my wrists. Just cut me."

So two of us held him down; one held his arms. I held his legs. Another of the guys grabbed a razor blade and made Swiss cheese out of his arms. Then we walked out, leaving him bleeding there in the cell.

Fortunately for Kid, within 25 minutes one of the guards walked by and found him. Normally, it takes several hours to die by slitting your wrists. He was rushed off to the hospital ward. We were all questioned about the incident, but claimed "we didn't see anything."

It was assumed by the big guns that Kid had done it to himself—that things just got too much for him and he went off the deep end. Kid showed up again in the block several months later. The only problem was: he couldn't lift his arms anymore. They just kind of dangled at his sides, limp. Just looking at him with his arms aimlessly bouncing at his sides made our stomachs turn. All of us were traumatized by it. You could see it in our eyes. Which one of us would crack next? Since none of us could stand to have Kid in the cell anymore, he ended up relocating with another bunch of guys.

* * * * * *

By Christmastime 1973, the men at McNeil had begun to grow resentful of being confined during the holidays. The racial tension was getting rough also. Brawls occurred almost daily—sometimes several times a day.

But one dinner hour, as I ate the usual, tasteless cafeteria food, the anger of all the prisoners seemed to explode all at once, as though someone had just struck a match to some gasoline.

A massive Chinaman—a guy about 6'6" and well over 200 pounds, who spent a lot of time at the iron pile—sauntered in as we were eating. As he approached, he slipped out a jagged bit of metal that had been made into a crude knife. For reasons no one knew except himself, he walked down the aisle of tables and stopped by a black guy eating across from me. Without a word, the Chinaman raised the knife and plunged the jagged edge into the black inmate's throat! Then he spun around and walked calmly out of the lunchroom, without so much as a backward glance. The poor black dude fell to the floor gasping for air. Within seconds he was dead.

None of us moved. We just kept eating as he gasped his last moment of life. All of us assumed he had it coming.

Guards descended on the cafeteria. Every prisoner in the room was questioned and requestioned. When the guard came to me, I just sneered at him. "I didn't see nothin.' I'm just sittin' here, eatin' my prison food, Man. Who'd want to miss out on any of this good stuff? I didn't see nothin'. I'm just eatin' my beans and drinkin' my coffee."

That night, I couldn't remember how much heroin I'd snorted or how many pills I'd swallowed. By this time, I was hitting dope every day. When we partied, I was known to be able to handle about five snorts at a time.

Seeing a guy's wrists slashed and watching the black guy fall to his death took their toll. I could feel myself beginning to melt from the inside out. I realized I wasn't so ice cold after all. I began to worry about myself. After all, drugs could take me only so high. At some point, I still had to face this fear. *What had I done with my life? How long was I going to live? Was I the next guy to get his throat slashed?* Deep inside, I was beginning to face facts and reality: I was alone, and I was afraid.

Then, one day, a riot broke out. No one really knew how it got started. Someone said some Chicanos had it in for the Black gang, who supposedly did in one of their guys. Before we knew it, the whole place had erupted. It hit the papers all over the United States. After it was all over, I could remember Jess and me holding up a bed mattress when the fuzz hosed us down with the fire hose. This was so we wouldn't be knocked down and get our innards blown out by the force of the water striking us.

Guys were running pell-mell in all directions. Shots were fired into the air. It was a horrifying scene. The subsequent lock down sure put a big crimp in our drug business. Getting comfortable was getting harder and harder. For months, we were watched closer than ever. For many months, it was a gray, bland, dismal prison life.

* * * * * *

Situated in the exercise yard of McNeil Prison was a level area, about two football fields long, which was surrounded by a high, chain-link fence topped with barbed wire. You could see out through the fence to Puget Sound. One of my more popular pastimes was to sit out on the bleachers and watch the killer whales blow spray through their blowholes. I also spent many hours watching the boats glide by, imagining I was free to sail the oceans of the world. However, I had only to turn and look behind me to be jarred back into the harsh reality of my hated confinement I could hardly call life.

Three gun towers stood guard over the recreation rectangle. The yard included a baseball diamond, a track that served also as a football field, several outdoor handball courts and a grassy area that had been turned into a miniature golf course. At the north end was a wooden platform known as the iron pile. That was where we lifted weights.

Things had settled down enough for me to make a drug delivery to the shed where the sports equipment was stored. Then I planned to head over to the iron pile. On the way, an old man collared me, calling me over by name. He'd been at McNeil since the '30s.

"Ron, I have something to tell you," said the old man.

I turned to glance at him, deciding whether or not I would talk to him. In the joint, men who don't know each other are very cautious about starting up any conversations, especially after a long lock down. Guys were usually looking for scapegoats or finks to do in, and dirty deals usually took place. Drug stashes disappeared; so did money. Nobody really knew if it was the prison fuzz or rival, competitive enterprisers who stole one another's stuff. Everyone's nerves were on edge.

The talk around the joint was that the old man had "gotten religion." However, the old cons are also highly respected. After all, a guy didn't live that long for nothing. So, if an old con wanted to talk to you, you generally gave him your ear. I decided I would oblige him.

He was tall and slender, with bent shoulders, but he held his chin high. His very being demanded respect. His eyes bore a deep look of serenity and peace—something unusual in the joint. His weatherbeaten face was leathery and crossed with deep lines that reflected years of anguish and abuse.

I didn't know the old man's name, but I didn't think I should interrupt him to ask. When I was about two feet from him, he continued, "Ron, I've been thinking about you. I've been in this joint since 1937, and I can tell you're a smart man. I'll tell you something else. We've got the best of everything in here—the best safecrackers, the best forgers. You can be anything you want to be in here. Did you know there's a guy in here who's a Napoleon? We've got a Lincoln. We've got an LBJ. We've got any kind of nut you can imagine. We've also got the best counterfeiters. They're all here, aren't they, Ron?"

I really didn't know how to answer, so I simply said, "Yeah, McNeil's got the craziest and the best of them, Old Man." I couldn't figure out what he was getting at.

"But, Ron, if you want to do some learning about peace, there's only one place to learn. You've got to look in this Book."

He held out a black book, which I recognized to be a Bible. I hesitated a moment. I didn't want to be seen taking anything from the old man, and I didn't know if I even wanted to touch a Bible. I wasn't sure what would happen if I did. Maybe God would strike me dead, or the ground would open up if I actually accepted it. I'd held one only once—way back in Sunday School—when Ma encouraged me to attend. The small mining town church, however, was hardly inviting to me. I never went back.

That black Book reminded me of Pop's cries about the hypocrites in the mining towns. Yet, way down deep, there was something about that Book that demanded my respect.

"Take it, Boy." His voice was gentle but firm. "You can look in it and learn about peace. You can look in it and get hold of Jesus. You know, He loves you, Son. I ain't never gettin' out of here. There's nothing left for me. This is why I'm here—to point out the way to Jesus to guys like you. Ron, you can make it. Ron, God's got something better for you."

Hesitantly, I reached out and took the Bible, quickly shoving it inside my jacket so no one would see it. Without another word, the old man turned and walked away. We never spoke again. In fact, I never saw him again. I took the Book back to my cell and hid it under my mattress; I didn't want any of my other cellmates to find it.

A few days later, I pulled the little Book out and tried to read. I looked first at a few Psalms; then I read a few Proverbs. They didn't really make any sense at all to me. I even tried to read the first chapter of Genesis. When I found a spot that listed some begats, I thought, "This is ridiculous! Maybe I'm not smart enough to understand it." I could only read at a third-grade level, so it was very frustrating, and each time I tried, I would end up shoving the Book back under my mattress in exasperation.

But the problem was that when I laid down there was this lump under my mattress that reminded me of the Book. It also reminded me of the old man's encouraging words. "Ron, there's something better for you."

It was a message of hope. Deep down, in the core of my heart where there was so much fear, hatred and loneliness, this little message of hope was also rolling around:

"Ron, there's something better for you."

I was afraid to believe it could be true. One morning, when I tried to read, I started with the first chapter of John, the Gospel of John. Again, in frustration, I began to curse myself. I threw the Book across the cell. But after a minute of silence, I decided I'd better pick it up before the others returned. If they saw it, they would think I'd "gotten religion" too.

I was sure I was cracking up. After all, Iceman didn't pay any attention to this kind of stuff. If the other guys knew it, they'd take me out for sure. I'd lose it all—all that status I'd taken such care to build up in the pen. I'd be known as a softy. I couldn't have that. That wouldn't exactly be the safest way to live in the joint if the guys thought I'd gone soft and "gotten religion." They'd nail me, for sure. I guess the only guy who'd talk to me, then, would be the old man.

When I stooped down to pick up the Book, it fell open to the sixth chapter of Isaiah and my eyes fell on the verse: "Then I heard the voice of the Lord saying, 'Whom shall I send? And who will go for us?' And I said, 'Here am I. Send me!'" (v. 8, *NIV.*)

I gently placed the Bible back under my mattress. Does this mean you can actually *hear* the voice of God? The thought intrigued me. Here's a guy, named Isaiah, who said he heard the voice of God, and God wanted to send him somewhere. I thought about this for several days. Can a guy like me really talk to God? I kept turning this thought over in my mind.

For several days after that, when walking across the yard, I kept hoping I'd run into the old man again. I didn't want to do anything to seek him out, because the guys would want to know why I wanted to see the old man. But the thought kept haunting me: Can God really talk to man? Can Ron Rearick and God really talk to each other?

One afternoon, while lying on my bunk, after my stint at the hospital, I shifted the Bible under my mattress to a slightly more comfortable spot, trying to forget it. It didn't work.

I decided to take a walk through the yard. I found myself muttering aloud. "Stop it! Leave me alone!" *Whom was I talking to? Was I going mad?* I decided to try an experiment. That night, I would try to talk to God. I'd remembered seeing a few movies where guys prayed. Anybody I'd ever seen praying was on their knees, so I figured that was the way it had to be done.

Lights Out came at 10:30, but we usually didn't drop off to sleep for hours. Sleep is a precious commodity behind bars, and no one does anything to disrupt another inmate's sleep. We managed to keep ourselves fairly busy during the days, but at night, when it's all silent, we just lie there in the dark, all alone. That's when the future has a way of closing in. Drugs were the only way we knew to put a troubled mind to sleep.

I lay there, waiting for the moment when my experiment could begin. I waited until there was no more rustling in the bunks around me. It must have been about 1:00 A.M. when I decided it was all clear for me to slip out of bed. I knelt down on the cold cement floor, listening for a long moment to determine if anyone else was rustling; I didn't want anyone to know about my experiment.

I took hold of the black bars and bowed my head. The light was streaming in from the hall, so I closed my eyes. I began to whisper, hoping the night guard and my cell buddies wouldn't hear me.

"Lord, if you're real and if uou really are who these

guys say you are, can you take this mess and do something with it?"

I held my breath and listened. Lightning didn't strike. My bunk didn't catch on fire. Nothing. I couldn't hear a sound. In my whole life, I couldn't remember this kind of silence. Maybe that was the sign I was supposed to get.

I listened again for a few moments—more intently this time. Nothing stirred. I started to pray again.

"God, please help me. I know I'm a real mess, but I'm starting to lose it. Iceman is melting. I know you're probably real busy, but could you just take a moment and help me?"

I was startled by the realization that I, the rough and tough Iceman, was actually talking to God. Just then, one of the other guys stirred. Startled, I literally jumped back into bed.

I got mad at myself for being so chicken, but I didn't want to be laughed at or put down, because I knew the other guys in my cell wouldn't understand. After all, I wasn't even sure if this business about God was totally real yet myself.

When my bunkmate settled down again, I got back on my knees and grabbed hold of the bars. When I heard someone moving down the hall, I jumped back into bed again. I laid there a moment, cursing. *What was I doing anyway? Was I scared that someone would catch me?*

I didn't seem to be able to help myself, because as soon as things settled down again, I was back on my knees. It seemed as though this Presence had entered my cell and had filled every fiber of my being! I knew then that the Lord was, indeed, real, though I didn't get zapped by lightning nor did my bed catch on fire.

I began to weep. Try as I might to stifle them, the sobs

just seemed to well up from within my depths. Many, many years of frustration, anger, fear, guilt and hatred seemed to roll out of me. I even found myself confessing things I'd done that no one else even knew about. I didn't know why.

Then I laid back on my bed and cried some more. No one stirred. I prayed and prayed for hours. A sense of calm finally overtook me, a sense of well-being flowed over me. At last, in thankfulness, I closed my eyes and slept like a baby, for the first time in years.

The next morning, when I awoke, still feeling God's love and forgiveness, the whole world looked different somehow. And something was even more amazing: The Presence was still there in my cell! All that day, I walked around with a silly grin on my face.

I decided I was going to find the old con who had earlier pressed the Bible into my hands.

I didn't even know his name. He hadn't introduced himself and I didn't think to ask. I was filled with questions about the Presence now in my life. But when I asked about him, someone in the yard said that several older men had been transferred to Leavenworth Penitentiary in Kansas. Days later, I finally had to give up the search. *Who knows? Maybe he was an angel.*

I didn't really know what to do with this whole scenario, but found myself trying to read the Bible. With my third-grade reading ability, it was sure rough going. Then I discovered that the New Testament was a little easier to understand.

I didn't stop drinking, smoking or taking drugs right off, but for some reason it occurred to me that I couldn't sell drugs anymore. So I handed my business over to Jess and the other guys. Thereafter, I took drugs only when someone happened to be passing a joint around in the cell, or some pills were being shared by my cellmates.

Actually, my life wasn't a whole lot different at first, yet it *seemed* as though everything was totally different. I just couldn't understand it; it was downright creepy, but every day my heart was definitely getting warmer and warmer.

Iceman was gradually melting down into a puddle.

15

Released!

For several months I lived, more or less, in a daze. I didn't really talk to anybody about what was going on inside me. One morning, I was standing at the mirror, extremely interested in how much easier it was to look at myself now. I didn't seem to hate myself anymore. I was carefully shaving around my mustache, when a guard came and rattled my cell door.

"Get ready to go, Rearick. We're sending you back to Salt Lake City."

In dismay, I turned to stare at him. *Was this guy joking, or what?* "What'd you say, Man?"

"Come on, Rearick. Get ready. The warden wants to see you," he repeated, obviously irritated.

I found myself standing in the warden's office, staring at the man in utter confusion.

"Warden, why am I being shipped back to Salt Lake?"

"I have no idea, Rearick. All I know is that Judge Ritter's calling you back to court."

I spent that night in an isolation cell. When a veteran con is going to be transported somewhere, the warden likes to separate him from his cell block the night before, and then move him quickly so there's no chance to lay escape plans along the way.

That night in the cell, I kept asking myself, "Why on earth am I going back to Salt Lake City? What's goin' on?"

I had called Van Heusen, my lawyer, that afternoon, but he had simply told me, "This is highly unusual, Ron. I don't know, it doesn't look good to me. I think they may have decided to add to your sentence because of other crimes. They caught Vic Galli, your old buddy, you know. They pinned a tax evasion charge on him. Who knows? He may have turned over some evidence against some of you lessers in his organization so you would have to do some time, too. I'll call Phil, but I don't think he knows anything either."

For me it was a long, quiet night. The next morning they shackled and bolted me to the floor of the car, and we headed out for Salt Lake City. The view along the way seemed more beautiful than I ever noticed before. The guards even seemed a little more decent than when I was brought to McNeil.

Along the way, I was smoking a cigarette and accidentally dropped it on the floor. I was afraid we'd all burn up before it could be retrieved from where it had rolled under the front seat. It took me a long time just to convince the fuzz we really had a problem. It wasn't 'til smoke began to curl up from beneath the seat that they finally believed me and pulled over.

It was really quite a sight. Here I was, in shackles, being held at gunpoint by one fuzz by the side of the freeway, while the other tried to find the smoldering cigarette. It was pretty comical, but also embarrassing.

Cars slowed down and people gawked at me. I felt like

a sideshow in a circus. I felt shame for the first time in my life. It kind of scared me. When it came time to return to the car, I slipped off into my own thoughts, trying to sort out what these feelings of both shame and peace meant— how they mixed together in my heart. Just then, the guard tapped me on the shoulder. "Rearick, are you okay? Come on, Man, we've got quite a ways to go yet."

With that, my mind shifted back to the present where I was chained to the floor of the backseat. The police car had just crossed the Utah border, when a news item blared from the car radio. I couldn't believe it! My mind exploded with emotion as I listened to the report: "This morning, the Honorable Judge Willis Ritter suffered a heart attack in his Salt Lake City home. Ritter served on the Federal Board for 21 years. He is listed in critical condition at the University Hospital."

Judge Ritter? A heart attack? It can't be. Here was the very man I'd threatened to murder just a few, short years ago, who was now going to die of a heart attack before I could find out why he wanted me back in his courtroom. I felt sick.

One of the guards turned to me, "Well, Rearick, this could be interesting. It looks like the Old Man's going down before you get there. Lucky for you, huh?"

I just nodded numbly. I didn't know what to say, yet I found myself wanting to pray for the man. In fact, I began to silently pray for the Hanging Judge. The man who'd sentenced me to 25 years and had marked me as "an habitual criminal" was now dying. It looked as though I could be vindicated if he died, yet, here I was praying that he would live. A mystery, to be sure.

The first person I'd ever prayed for in my life was the judge who had sent me to prison and whom I'd threatened to kill. This thought didn't strike me 'til several days later, when I was in a cell at the Salt Lake City Jail pondering what might possibly happen to me next. Life certainly seemed to be getting confusing to me. It seemed to have been taken totally out of my hands.

Maybe other people experienced God's reality like this guy Isaiah I kept reading about. Maybe I was going to be able to help Judge Ritter somehow. "Naw! I can't even help myself!" I muttered, as I fell asleep.

Several weeks went by. No one really knew what to do with me. I did learn that the judge was recovering, however, and was amazed that he planned to resume his court duties within a matter of days. So, after about four weeks in the Salt Lake City Jail, there I was, once again standing before the bench of the Hanging Judge.

The judge looked quite frail. His face was a little sunken. This time he wasn't smiling. In fact, he looked somewhat mystified. He gazed at me and, in a weak voice, asked the court clerk, "Clerk, what's this man doing in my courtroom?"

"I don't know, Your Honor," replied the clerk.

Judge Ritter then turned to my attorneys. "Can you gentlemen tell me what this man is doing back in my courtroom?"

"No, we can't, Your Honor," spoke Mr. Van Heusen, for both of them.

"No, you don't know," answered the judge strangely. "No one knows why he's here, except me, and I'm not sure that *I* even know why."

Judge Ritter turned to me. "Son, I've called you back to my court for one reason. One night, several weeks ago, I just found it in my heart to call you back and give you a pardon. I'm going to give you one more chance, and you'd better make the best of it, Son. Someone up there likes you for some reason, and there's something better for you than prison. So, let's put some effort into finding what it is! You're pardoned and released!"

Two hours later, I was out on the streets of Salt Lake City—a *free man!* I was stunned. My legs shook. I could hardly breathe. Pardoned! I kept repeating. "Pardoned by the Hanging Judge!" I had to pinch myself to believe it. It had really happened.

I knew better than to try to contact the judge to thank him. Federal criminals are never allowed to have anything to do with the prosecutor or the judge involved in their case. The FBI usually keeps a good eye on released cons for just this reason. They often shoot first and ask questions later.

It was truly beyond comprehension. It was definitely a miracle, yet I knew I didn't deserve it. I was completely stunned by the whole process. God really had gone to bat for me, Ron Rearick, the guy who would "never amount to anything."

Only a month earlier, I was just a number at McNeil Island Penitentiary. Now, I was a free man with a number.

I shuffled into the parole office and registered my Mom's address as my residence. I decided to settle in there for a couple of days to figure out what to do next.

My release from prison remained a mystery.

16

First Steps

It was great to be back in Mom's home for a while. She, of course, was sure her son was just an innocent victim all along. Some of the family dropped by, and all my friends kept saying, "It's a miracle!" I even used the term myself, but said it with much depth and respect. It had a ring of truth to it that made me want to say it respectfully. I would simply answer, "Yes, it's a miracle."

When I got up the next morning, I knew it would be so easy to set up my dope business again. A phone call was all it would take. All I'd have to do is call a guy and he'd bring me a weapon and a carload of dope, and I'd be back in business, as quick as a wink. Before long, I'd be living again in the style I always wanted.

Yet, inside, I just knew it wasn't for me. I knew God had set me free from prison and I owed Him a whole lot, if I could just figure out what He wanted me to do for Him. But I knew I owed Him, and the thought haunted me.

I soon got a job at a truck-loading dock. This time, though, I wasn't there to steal from my employer. I quickly became one of the best employees in the company—a big change for me. I still attended a few parties and smoked a little pot now and then. In fact, my coke habit was getting right up there where it had been in the joint, just a few months earlier. I was meeting a few chicks, too. Things seemed to be going well for me.

But I never seemed to get away from this thought: "What does God want me to do for Him?" I'd been struggling my way through a few books I'd bought at a Bible bookstore. Once, I even stumbled into the back of a church. I don't really remember what kind it was, but I do remember trying to sit through the service. It was frustrating because I understood so very little of what was going on, and no one seemed to be too interested in my being there.

I found my way home, and decided that God and I must have a corner on what He had in mind for me, because I certainly didn't fit in that church. One night, it came to me. It was the Almighty God who had set me free. I planned to attend a dope party that night, so I decided I would tell everybody there what God had done for me.

By this time, the mid-1970s, the Jesus People had been in Salt Lake City parks for several years. I had watched them do what they called *witnessing*. I noticed they handed out pieces of paper and did little raps about what the Lord meant to them. I figured I could handle that. In fact, I'd already told a few guys in the park about Jesus. I'd even taken one of my paychecks and bought a stack of tracts, and then walked up and down handing them out. I had also managed to get a few people to give their hearts to the Lord.

I had a unique way of witnessing in those early days. One guy took a tract from me, then crumpled it up and threw it on the ground. It really burned me up to see him wasting God's money like that! After all, God had given me the money to get that tract, and this guy was being disrespectful. I grabbed the guy by the throat, threw him on the ground and started hitting him a few times. I told him he was going to receive Jesus, or else, and that he wasn't going to blaspheme the Lord anymore.

Whenever I was in the park, I noticed the Jesus People seemed to flee; some hid behind trees. Ironically, a few years later, I ran into one of the guys I had "beaten into the faith." He remembered the story with humor and respect.

At the dope party that night, I decided to tell my old buddy Brad about Jesus. Brad had a real serious drug problem, and he needed to know about the miracle God did for me.

I walked in a little late, as it'd taken me a few swings around the block to bolster up my courage. I knew what I had to do. I had to tell my friends about God. By the time I got there, the party was well underway. Brad, the chicks and a few other guys had already snorted a few lines of coke and were revved up pretty high.

Sitting down next to Brad, I said, "Brad, God's told me to tell you something. You know, it was He who set me free."

Brad just looked at me and said, "Okay, Man, so God set you free. Great!"

"You know, Brad, God really wants to set you free, too. All you have to do is just talk to Him; give Him your heart. That's all I did. I just talked to Him, and I read His Book once in a while. Now I'm a free man. I've experienced a miracle, and so can you, Brad."

"Okay, Man, yeah. I'll give it a try sometime. Thanks, Ice," Brad replied patronizingly as he walked away.

I spent most of the evening roving from room to room at the party, smoking a couple of joints and looking for more opportunities to tell people about God. Later on, as I walked from the kitchen into the living room, I overheard Brad talking to another of my buddies.

"Man, you can't believe what's happened to Iceman. The guy's tellin' me I need to give my heart to God."

The other guy leaned back laughing, and said, "Yeah, I've heard he's got religion; but hey, just offer him a little coke, some smack, maybe a joint. He'll shut up. He'll forget this Jesus stuff. He's got religion for a little while. It happens to a lot of people. Just watch. It won't last long."

It was just like a knife being thrust into my heart. Is that what they think about my God? Is that what they think about me? What hurt the most is that I knew it was true. They honestly believed that drugs controlled my life, not God. They honestly didn't take me seriously, and that hurt the most.

They were treating me like some crazy. They didn't understand at all. Something had to be done. That night, when I went home, I knelt down for the second time in my life and talked to God. I knew this was going to be hard, real hard. After 12 years of addiction, the craving for drugs—particularly coke—was getting more and more intense. I knew that the hardest thing in the world for me would be to live without my dope, but I also knew I had to. So I knelt down and cried out to God.

"God, I still don't understand what you want with my life. I can't quit taking drugs on my own. I need a fix. I can't leave the chicks alone either. There's just something inside me that craves both of them. God, if you can help me, I'll live right."

Again, the same Presence that had filled my cell at

McNeil Island Penitentiary filled the room as I knelt down by the couch—with a soft carpet instead of cold cement under my knees. The same Presence filled my heart. The same quiet peace flowed through me. I knew I was finally free.

* * * * * *

In addition to my other bad habits, I'd always had the temper of three demons. No one liked to mess with me. The next few weeks proved to be real rough, because I'd decided to quit smoking too. That, along with not taking any drugs and leaving the chicks alone, made me extra irritable.

One of the guys at the yard started joshing me about having a Bible in my lunch bag. That burned me up. Besides, the guy was a real twerp; I never did have much use for him. Now, here he was verbally pushing me around about reading the Bible, and calling me a "Bible boy." After two or three days of this, I decided it was time for him to find out just what a Bible boy could do to him.

It was a Thursday, at noontime. We were all in the lunchroom. As I walked by his table, the twerp stuck his foot out and tried to trip me. Instead of falling, I banged into the wall and bruised my shoulder.

"Hey, Man, what do you think you're doin'?"

The twerp replied, "I wanted to see if a Bible boy can control his temper."

I lunged at him, snarling, "Yeah? The Bible boy can control his temper. I can control it long enough to tear you to pieces!"

I began swinging with a flurry of punches. He was stunned and completely taken off guard. Everyone cleared out of the room. I slid him down the table, picked him up and began banging his head against the wall. My rage almost blinded me.

Someone started tugging at my shoulder urgently. "Hey, Ice, stop it! You're going to kill him! Man, you're going to kill him!"

He didn't really have to pull me away, because, for several seconds, I had already been aware of what I was doing. It was as though I'd been lifted out of my body and was looking down at the fight. It was just long enough to let me see the ugliness of my temper. I stopped, picked the poor guy up and began to cry. "Hey, Man, forgive me! I'm sorry, Man! I'm really sorry!"

The guy did forgive me. The other guys couldn't believe it—Ice was crying. I was shocked too. I'd never said I'm sorry to anybody in my life. It looked like the Lord and I had another battle to work out. My anger had to go.

I'd never heard the word *repentance* before, but I did understand the warm feeling I had when I asked the dude to forgive me. It was such a nice, warm feeling, but hard to explain. I'd always been so afraid of the words *forgive me*. The astonished looks on the faces of my co-workers seemed to matter to me, all of a sudden. I knew a couple of them now thought I was a sissy. Even I thought I might be cracking up. What bothered me was the other guys probably figured I was really afraid of going back to the joint. I knew it was more than that.

I also got a chance to ask Mom to forgive me. In fact, we sat down one day and had a good long talk. I began to explain to her about this new thing that was happening in my heart. It was great talking to her about it, because she always got so excited about anything I was enthused about. At first, though, it seemed hard for her to understand what I was talking about, but she could certainly tell there was a change in me.

When it came time to move out on my own, I felt sad; a new love and tenderness towards Mom and my sisters was growing in my heart—feelings I'd never experienced before. It seemed like, all at once, I realized that *I* wasn't the center of the universe. Others became important to me.

The simple phrases *Would you forgive me* and *I'm sorry,* began to grow like seeds in my heart. Their effect seemed to blossom and spread throughout my personality. Each morning when I got up and looked in the mirror it seemed as though my eyes were beginning to look softer. Even the slight glow of a smile began to appear. "I'm sorry, Lord," began to be spoken from my heart regularly. I was becoming a *bigger* person.

* * * * * *

Eventually, I found my way to a Baptist church. They were a pretty straight group of people. Because I kept hearing that a Christian is supposed to go to church, every Sunday I'd put on my best clothes and head down to the little church. At first, I sat in the back row, but the group was small enough that soon I was known by everyone attending. Having been an ex-convict, I was something of a novelty. Everybody wanted me over to their home.

The pastor was most interested in me. This particular church had about 30 members, and a list of the members was posted behind the pulpit. Each Wednesday, the list was brought out. Next to each name was the number of people he or she had brought to church. I remember one gal, Sally, who had brought as many as 20 to 30 people.

One Sunday, the pastor read down the list, mentioning that two or three had done very well that week. When he came to my name, he noted I hadn't brought anybody to church. Though gentle, his comment pricked me.

"Maybe, one of these days, we'll get Ron on the stick. He'll start bringing some people into the church as well. Ron, we're all praying for you. We know Jesus wants to use you."

Well, that's all I needed. I wasn't going to let these folks take me out. I was going to be the best "church-bringer" they ever had. By now, I'd learned a bit of tact in witnessing. But I still figured, from reading the Old Testament, that the Lord used a lot of force to get things done. There seemed to be a lot of sword-slinging, and I particularly loved the story about Samson, who used a donkey's jawbone to slay all those Philistine dudes.

I knew I could handle that kind of thing. The way I figured it, if the Mafia could use me, why couldn't the Lord use me? After all, my muscles were the most valuable part of me. By now, I'd been hearing a lot about gifts. I'd also seen a man on TV, talking about all of us being gifted by the Spirit, so I figured my gift must be that of a "muscle man" for the Lord.

I decided to go to the park and pick up some dude to bring to church the next Sunday. When we walked in the door, the pastor pulled me aside and asked, "Ron, what happened to this young man?"

I grinned a smile that would have done wonders for a toothpaste ad and replied, "Well, he didn't want to come, Pastor, but he's here, and he's ready to listen."

After church, the pastor asked me to meet him for breakfast the next morning. During breakfast, he began to talk to me about this Person called the Holy Spirit.

"Do you know, Ron, that the Lord doesn't really need our works and efforts to do His work? He just asks us to be channels for His Spirit."

I had great difficulty understanding some sort of invisible Person inside me. But he gave me a number of Bible verses to study. We went through the Gospel of John, chapters 14-16, and we read some of the book of Acts. "Ron, you've got to trust the Holy Spirit to help you bring people. You can't go around using force anymore."

Eventually, I heard about a meeting involving a group of Christian businessmen. One of the guys in my church had started going to the meetings and thought I might like them too. I went a couple of times and got to know the Salt Lake City chapter of the Full Gospel Businessmen.

When they heard my story, I was invited to be a speaker at the next meeting. I was really excited about it. This was going to be my first opportunity to talk publicly about what had happened to me. The man in charge of the meeting said they expected 15 to 20 guys at the next meeting.

The following month, on a Saturday morning, I arrived about 10 minutes later than I was supposed to. It didn't matter. The guys were all wolfing down some pancakes, and they seemed to be having a great time talking.

When it came to prayer time and requests were taken, one of the guys was concerned that the Mormons were really influencing some of his family members. He asked that we pray that the young people wouldn't be taken in by what the Mormons say.

I'd never really given much thought to the Mormons around Salt Lake City, but when we began to discuss some books saying they were a cult, I knew what that meant. I listened as they talked. It seemed they were really irritated about the Mormons. At a quiet point in the meeting, I raised my hand and offered a solution.

"Hey, I know how to handle those dudes. I've got some guys who are into powder. The way I see it, if we take out their temple, we'll discourage them enough they'll probably want to leave Salt Lake—you know, something like Jericho."

Their jaws all dropped open. There was dead silence. Right then, I knew I'd said something wrong, but I didn't rightly know what. After all, my plan seemed to make a lot more sense than any they'd talked about. The moderator broke in at that point. "Yeah, Ron, right. We'll give that some consideration."

I could tell they were surprised I was serious in my suggestion.

I gave my testimony that morning, but the guys seemed to have a hard time handling what I said. Though obviously excited to hear how I'd met the Lord in my cell at McNeil Prison, they were also cautious about being too enthusiastic. After the meeting, one of the vice presidents pulled me aside to talk to me about the love of God.

Taking my arm, he said, "Do you know, Ron, how God really does His work?"

"Yeah, He does it with His power," I answered.

He continued, "Not exactly. Do you know how He touched you in that penitentiary? That Presence you felt was the love of God. The book of Romans tells us about the love of God that's shed abroad in our hearts. God's going to love you so much, Ron, that you'll start to love others; and people, like the Mormons, will learn to love God through you when they see the love you have for them. But you can't go around blowing them up, or even talking about it. Instead, God's going to teach you a whole new way of life, Ron. He's got something a lot better for you."

In those early days, I was truly learning a lot about how things were to be different for me. It seemed like everything that had worked so well for me in the past was not the way it was to be done in the future. I began to catch on that if Ron Rearick was going to make it as a Christian, he was going to have to decide to be a learner.

I was just starting to get this down, when I heard a message about what it was to be a disciple. For the first time in my life, I was now interested in learning what others had to say to me, instead of forcing my ways on everyone else.

17

A New Way—A New Love

One Saturday, I decided to go to the park and watch how the Jesus People witnessed. These kids were quite a bit younger than I, and they dressed a little funny, as far as I was concerned.

I purchased a handful of tracts to give away. While walking through the park, I handed a tract to a group of three students. One of them glanced at the tract, crumpled it up and threw it on the ground. That really burned me up. I reached down, picked it up, handed it back to him and said, "Hey, Man, straighten up and read it, right now, in front of me!"

His two buddies just walked on, trying to avoid the situation. The kid was obviously shaken. I decided I was going to break through to him; I was going to teach him to respect God. After he had time to read the tract, I asked, "Now, are you ready to receive Christ? Are you ready to do the four steps and respond to it?"

The guy just looked at me dumbfounded, and said: "Hey, Man, who are you kidding? Get off my back!"

With that, I grabbed him by the throat and slammed

him up against a tree, my voice rising in anger. "Are you ready to receive Christ? Or are you going to burn in hell, punk?"

Scared out of his wits, he responded, "Yeah, Man, whatever you want, whatever you want."

I cuffed him on the side of his head a couple of times and told him to kneel down and pray with me.

About that time, one of the Jesus People came out from behind a tree. Shaking his finger in my face, he said, "Hey, Man, you're way out of line and you're an embarrassment to the gospel!"

That really shook me up. I was ready to hit him. I couldn't understand what I'd done wrong. After all, wasn't this Christian guy supposed to be on my side? "Let him go! Come on. I'll buy you a cup of coffee. My name's Ben."

As we sat down for coffee, I said, "Hey, Man, I've been pretty effective. People really do listen to me."

"Judging by your method, I'm sure they do. But did you ever wonder why they don't come back around?"

That had never really crossed my mind. Everything Ben said seemed to make sense. Right then and there, he took me through a little study in the book of Romans.

"Hey, Ron, you need to know the Person of the Spirit. It's the Holy Spirit who convinces people—not your force. It's the Holy Spirit who shines through you with the love of Jesus that makes people respond."

I nearly cried while talking to him, because that's what I really wanted. After all, I could not only believe what God had done for me, but I knew He wanted to do it for the whole world as well.

"So I need this Holy Spirit?"

"Yeah," replied Ben, "come to our Bible study tonight, across from the park. Pastor Jim will be there, along with a roomful of folks who have just given their hearts to the Lord. You can receive the Spirit there, too. I'll be there to help and pray with you."

I trusted Ben, so I said I'd be there that night. He seemed like a nice enough guy. We parted, saying we'd see each other at the meeting. Ben was the first man who had ever taken me seriously, who had taken the time to explain where I was wrong and how I could do things better in such a way that I didn't feel put down. From that time on, Ben and I became great friends.

I was now a learner. I liked the feeling.

* * * * * *

At this time one of my greatest prayers was to have a wife. Since my whole attitude about women had started to change shortly after I returned from prison, I began to see women in an entirely new light. I wanted to be married, but was hesitant because my last two marriages had failed. I really believed I could be a good husband now, for I was beginning to see that my past failures had not been the fault of the women I'd married, but my own.

I was very lonely and wanted to share my life with someone, but I didn't know quite what to do about it. One night, on TV, I heard a preacher say you could actually pray for a wife. It made sense to me. If I could pray in prison and be freed, and if I could be freed from drugs and smoking by praying about it, then why couldn't I ask God for a wife?

The man on the program said you could even make out a list of the kind of woman you wanted to marry. Your faith would be expressed as you wrote down specifically what you wanted. It sounded simple enough to me, so I made up my list. It went something like this: "Lord, I thank you that you've given me a wife (1) who is good looking, (2) who is smart, (3) who thinks I'm the smartest man in the whole world, (4) who has red hair, (5) who is a good cook and (6) who will accept and understand me after all I've been through."

I waited three days in frustration. There was no answer. I decided that I must not have enough faith yet and just forgot about it. I folded up my list and buried it deep in my Bible so no one would find it and just forgot about it.

* * * * * *

I went to the Bible study that night. I was a little nervous about a prayer meeting, as I wasn't sure if anybody knew about me and my past. I'd recently flunked out at Pastor Phillip's Baptist church, and I was sure everyone knew about it.

I had convinced Pastor Phillips that I should share a service with him. I thought that was appropriate, particularly as I'd heard a number of people in the congregation say they would like me to be the assistant pastor. After all, hadn't I also been quite effective in bringing people to Jesus?

It was quite a sermon, all right. I got up and spoke about Noah and the whale. I couldn't figure out all the snickers, but was fairly certain that it was something I had said, or maybe it was something I had forgot to do, so I checked my zipper two or three times while I kept on preaching. I knew I had something to say and I intended to say it.

After the service, Pastor Phillips gently pulled me back

into his office and informed me that it wasn't Noah who got swallowed by the whale. It was Jonah; it was Noah who had been boarded up in an ark.

"Son, I really don't think you ought to share publicly until you get a chance to learn the Bible. We love you a lot around here, Ron, but I just can't have you up there telling the Bible wrong. It's just flat embarrassing! You need to take some time and really study the Bible and learn what you're talking about."

I was sure stories had circulated all over town about the ex-con planning to blow up the Mormon temple and who didn't even know the difference between Noah and Jonah. I was getting real nervous around Christians. I always seemed to be putting my foot in my mouth and making a fool of myself, but I decided to go to the Thursday prayer meeting anyway. Besides, I felt I owed it to my new friend Ben, who really seemed to know his Bible stuff; I thought I could really learn a lot from him.

When I arrived, I walked back and forth in front of the house several times. Quite a few dudes were sitting on the porch; they looked like hippies. One guy, with a big old Bible wearing a white shirt with the sleeves rolled up to his elbows and beat-up hippy-type work boots, stood out front. I figured he must be trying to be some kind of preacher. They all looked at me as I walked by two or three times. Finally, one of them hollered out, "Hey, come on in."

"Is this where the prayer meeting is happening?" I hollered back.

Two of the young men left the porch and walked down the sidewalk toward me. One extended his hand. I reached out and shook the guy's hand, but kept him at a distance as we started up the stairs into the house.

There were young men and women all over the place—in the kitchen, in the living room and in dining area—all praying. I mean, they were praying *loud!* Many had their hands lifted. Others knelt, bowing their heads. I was mystified. Everything seemed just a little bit disoriented to me. I decided to sit in the corner, next to a small, brass lamp. I figured if anything got too weird, I'd just grab the lamp, thump a few of them on the head and run out.

But as the meeting progressed, I forgot about the lamp. I really began to get excited. These people were really, honestly touching God! I had knelt down and prayed before, but I'd never done anything like this. After prayer time, there was a time of sharing, Bible study, then more singing. I didn't sing too well, so I sang softly. In fact, my singing was so embarrassing, I hired a lady later on, at $30 an hour, to give me lessons.

It seemed as though these Christians did a lot of singing. Though I had a song in my heart after I became a Christian, it just didn't seem to come out of my mouth the same way it did for others. I really liked the fast choruses and I enjoyed clapping to the rhythms, so I sang softly and clapped loudly. It seemed to get me through the evening.

At the close of the meeting, the leader, the guy with the white shirt, rolled-up sleeves, jeans and work boots, stood up and asked if anybody wanted to have the Holy Spirit in their life or have hands laid on them. I knew this was why Ben asked me to come to the meeting—to receive the Spirit. He had come to the meeting later than I and was about three rows back. I tried not to look at Ben when the leader asked this. I was sure, by the way Ben was looking around, that he'd already set it up and that everybody there knew I was the one who came to get it. I was kind of self-conscious at this point.

Two guys slipped down on their knees on the floor and, before I knew it, six people were standing all around each of them, pressing hands on them and praying. *I don't know if I want to get in on this.* But before I knew it, it was like a force of some kind had taken hold of me, and I found myself down on my knees too, with five or six people praying over me.

I didn't understand a word being said by any of them. I was suddenly overwhelmed, once again, by the Presence of the Lord—the same kind of Presence that I had experienced on at least two other occasions. Without effort, I lifted my hands and poured out praise. I'd learned to repent. I'd learned to confess; and now, for the first time, I was really learning how to praise. Rivers, deep within my being, were being released—rivers expressing to God exactly what I thought. Now I understood why they liked to sing their choruses.

Later, I was told that I actually prayed in the Spirit in the same spot for over an hour! If I did, I was oblivious to the time; it seemed like only a moment to me. Then, finally, my heart became still.

I lifted my head and opened my eyes. There, directly in front of me, sat a lovely woman on the sofa, her eyes still closed in prayer. She was beautiful and petite, with blond curly hair, the kind I really liked, that fell down around her shoulders. As I stood in the afterglow of my praise experience, I caught myself staring at her. As yet, I hadn't met anybody who was both beautiful and loved the Lord Jesus—or perhaps I hadn't noticed before.

As I looked at her, I felt so clean inside. For the first time in my life, I found myself looking at a woman without any intention of sexual gratification. I was thinking only what a wonderful person she appeared to be. I became overwhelmed with the warmth of being able to think this way after so many years of sordid experiences with women.

At that moment, something startling happened deep within. I'd heard about God giving words and sentences to people, but I wasn't prepared for it to happen to me—at least not so soon in my walk with the Lord. But there it was, unmistakably, a voice that said, "Ron, you're looking at your helpmate."

I knew what the term *helpmate* meant; I'd heard it several times in church already. I knew what He meant; this woman was to be my wife! As I sat on the couch exchanging small talk with some of the guys, I kept glancing out of the corner of my eye at her. What should I do? Would the Lord want me to ask her, right now, to be my wife?

This was really a switch. Several times, I'd tried to get some of my old girlfriends saved and get them to church, but they just didn't seem to catch on. And here God was dropping a lovely, saved gal right into my lap, with no effort on my part. The Lord really does move in mysterious ways. But, after a moment of savoring this idea, I chided myself.

"Get hold of yourself, Ron. This gal is much too classy for you. If she ever found out who you were, she wouldn't like you anyway. You're just going to have to go back and get one of your old girlfriends saved and learn to live the way you're living now."

However, I could hardly control the excitement raging through me at that moment, just thinking about the possibility of marrying someone like this lovely creature I'd seen tonight for the first time. After I left the prayer meeting, without approaching her, I kicked myself all the way home, yet I also realized that you don't just walk up to some gal and say, "Hey, the Lord just told me you're supposed to marry me." I mean, even though I was a big hunk and knew I'd make a great husband. What do you do when you know you have a word from the Lord and that this was going to be your wife?

Three days later, Ben invited me for a Sunday night potluck. I went, hoping she would be there. When I walked in the door, I immediately turned red because I bumped right into her. There she was: the most beautiful gal in the world—and she loved Jesus! How lucky could I be!

I sat across the table from her and discovered that she was real easy to talk to. Soon, we were telling each other how we met the Lord and what we felt was in store for us. Her name was Margery Davis; she was 34, a single mom with a 10-year-old daughter named Dina. She was traveling with a woman evangelist, tutoring her children. They'd arrived in Salt Lake a few weeks earlier. In addition, she was warm, vivacious and her eyes were soft and gentle. I could tell she liked me.

I was sure this nice gal must have been a pastor's daughter and in church all her life; she seemed so pure. I just knew she'd probably never talked to an ex-pusher or ex-con like me before.

Toward the end of supper, I finally gathered the courage to ask her if I could see her again. What the heck, I figured, she might as well know what I had been. Sooner or later, she'd probably find out anyway from someone else. So I plunged in. "Could I see you again, Margery, that is, if you don't mind being with a guy who's been in prison most of his life? I've done a lot of time in the joint. I've seen a lot, done a lot and I've been off drugs only a few months, but I'm a real nice guy." I stopped and grinned.

164

Margie just looked up. "I'd love to get to know you, Ron."

The following Wednesday afternoon I knocked on the door of Marge's apartment. If she'd known how worked up I got over this whole thing, she probably wouldn't even open the door. I'd taken time off from work, just so I could get there in plenty of time to see her.

When she opened the door, I noticed she was dressed in pink. She looked so innocent and so alive. My heart pounded hard against my chest. I was very nervous. As the door opened, I had the strongest urge to run and never come back, because I was sure she'd never like me once she really got to know me.

Marge took my arm and sat me down at the table, where we each had a large glass of iced tea. My mouth was like the Sahara Desert between slurps of tea. I was so nervous, I gobbled up a whole plate of cookies, apologizing for eating so many, but kept right on eating them.

We had a great conversation that afternoon. It had been a week since I saw her at the prayer meeting. For that entire week, she had been in my thoughts constantly. Every time I opened the Bible, I saw her face looking up at me.

Several times, I tried to tell her about my past, but I always seemed to get interrupted. I mean, I really wanted to warn Margie. Here I was, a guy who'd hardly ever held down a decent job (most of them had been in illegal activities); I'd been a big-time drug dealer for a long time, and I probably wasn't safe to be around. Besides that, who knew what the Mafia would do to me if they found out I now had religion.

But each time I tried to explain to her about my past, she would interrupt me and change the subject. Finally, she said, "Ron, I know you're trying to warn me about yourself and I appreciate it. I already like you, Ron. You don't have to warn me. I think you'd better know something about my past as well."

Margie then began to share with me her story, about spending many years in a commune in the caves of northern California, about being the granddaughter of a Pentecostal preacher, about being a call girl in Las Vegas, about being a slave to heroin and about how her first child was killed beside the freeway while she just stood there in a drug stupor.

I was totally stunned as she talked. I couldn't believe that this lovely creature sitting on the couch with me, who had had just as many horrible experiences in life as I had, was now this wonderful, tender woman—a woman who reads the Bible, knows Jesus, is beautiful, childlike, with a strong peace in the Spirit! As she talked, I began to realize that there was hope for me also. If God could do all this for her, then He could make something out of my life as well. Suddenly, life took on a wonderful aura and looked much rosier for me than it had in a long, long time.

I also realized now what had been filling her heart when I had tried to tell her my story. So, the more she talked, the more I respected her, the more I loved her and the more I wanted to marry her. But I'd known her only a week. Thoughts swirled in my head. I was actually getting a little dizzy. Too much was happening at once, too much to absorb.

What should I do? I kept hearing the words: Ron, this is your helpmate. Yet, I didn't want to embarrass myself. This was all I needed to have get around town, along with what people already knew about me, that I planned to blow up the Mormon Temple, that I had Noah in the whale and now I was asking every gal I met to marry me. I was afraid she might laugh at me, too. That, I couldn't have handled.

A few more minutes of conversation went by, then these words just tumbled out: "Well, I guess we really couldn't hurt each other any more than we've already been hurt ourselves, could we, Marge?"

She laughed. "No, I don't think so, Ron."

I couldn't stand it any longer. Flushed red, I stood up, took both her hands in mine and, with gruffness that was intended to be tenderness, I looked intently at her and blurted out, "Woman, I want you to marry me!"

Oh, how I wished I could have caught those words before they were said and expressed them in a more gentle way. Instead, they'd erupted like some sort of demand. Why, oh why, couldn't I have said them better? I started again, stumbling over the words. "Uh, what I mean is . . . uh . . . Marge, I want you to marry me; that is, if you'd like to. I know we've known each other only a week, but would you marry me, Marge?"

Marge looked at me with a big, knowing grin that seemed to last an eternity. "Well, it's about time you asked me. I knew a week ago that you were going to ask me to marry you. I've just been praying for you, Ron."

We both laughed. She'd laugh, then I'd laugh, then we both cried. I pulled her up off the couch and gave her a great big kiss.

Within a week we were married in a little Baptist church. Rev. Jim Powers of the Full-Armor Fellowship assisted with the ceremony. Communion was served by Marge's friend, Rev. Pat Squire. The service seemed electrified. All our friends packed the small church. Both ministers gave wonderful sermons. Marge and I just stood sharing glances, grinning at each other, knowing that we now had a whole new, wonderful life ahead of us. When the service was over, I lifted my new wife up in my arms and spun her around at the altar. Everyone stood up with shouts of joy!

There was an interesting mix of people at the church—all my new church friends, Marge's friends from the prayer fellowship and my new daughter Dina. A number of my old street buddies stood perplexed—almost apprehensive—in the midst of all the hallelujahs and praise to the Lord, all the hugging and cheers, not knowing what to make of all this joy.

Again, I felt that same Presence, the One I'd felt at McNeil Island; again, when I was freed from drugs; and still again, when I received the Holy Spirit. I knew now that same Presence would inhabit our home as well. I turned around and stepped off the altar with a great sense of assurance, knowing that all was now well. As we walked up the aisle and outside the church, our friends threw rice at us, shouted and cheered.

A man I barely knew walked over and slipped a $20 bill in my hand. "Ron, I didn't know what to bring as a present, but my wife and I want you to have a great honeymoon. We thought this would buy you at least one nice meal on your honeymoon."

I looked down at the $20 in my hand, thanked the man and gave him a great big bear hug. I was so deeply touched by the gift. "Oh, brother, that will be more than enough!"

I handed it to Marge. All the time I was thinking, "I can look down at this $20 bill and feel *so* content. I'm so happy. In the past, I would have said that it wasn't enough; but now, it's more than enough. It's more than what we will need."

For a few seconds, I remembered back to just four

years earlier, when I held a million dollars in my hand and cried out: "It's *not* enough!" Leaning over to Marge, I said: "Marge, you know what I'm feeling right now? That $20 bill was a real sign for me."

"How's that?"

"Well, just four years ago, I had a million dollars in my hands and I screamed out, cursing God, that He hadn't given me enough!"

Marge gasped and looked at me quizzically. "A million dollars?! What did you do to get a million dollars?"

I turned to her. "Marge, I've got a lot of things to tell you about. It'll probably take me a whole lifetime." Then we headed out.

Our first night, we decided to read the Bible together. When I opened my Bible, the little piece of paper on which I'd written my list a few months earlier while watching the TV evangelist slipped out onto the floor. I picked it up. I was embarrassed and didn't want Marge to see it. Quietly, I chuckled as I read down the list. I'd asked for a redhead, for someone who could accept me and understand me and who was a good cook.

I crumpled the piece of paper and tossed it into the wastebasket. Marge asked, "What are you doing?"

Sheepishly, I answered, "Oh, nothin'. Marge, you're really a good cook, aren't you, . . . and you're so beautiful!"

18

Icebergs

Marge and I had a great life together. And for the first time in my life, I enjoyed being a father. It was even more than I could imagine. Having someone call me Dad and pray for me was quite an experience. Dina was a great kid and I enjoyed being around her, watching out for her, doing things with her. Marge and I never had an argument and it seemed we were made for each other. One day I told her, "It's like the Lord knew all along that we would need each other."

Every time Dina called me Dad, I saw myself in a different light. I mean, she really wanted me to be her dad. She wanted me to be her protector and provider. I told everyone that Marge was a great mom, but I was too shy to say I was a great dad.

Even though I'd come to know Jesus in a new and wonderful way, there was still one person I found it extremely hard to pray for: old Smiley Rearick, my dad. From time to time, I experienced nightmares about him—his voice echoing out from the past, contrasting harshly with all the good things I was now experiencing.

Though everyone liked me, in the middle of the night I would hear: "Ron Rearick, you're *no* good. You're *never* going to amount to anything." I'd awaken in a cold sweat, but still feeling the impact of Pop speaking to me. It was as though he was saying, "Ron, you're *not* going to make it. You're not good enough for God."

At times, I'd wake up, clutching the side of the bed, hoping I wouldn't awaken Marge. When this had gone on for a while, I sensed that the Holy Spirit wanted to do another deep work in me. I knew I had to make peace with Pop, even though he had long since died.

We were now part of a church. In fact, within six months, Marge and I became elders in a group of street people, now Christians. Unfortunately, there were too many chiefs and not enough Indians. Most of us had come from real rough backgrounds and had begun to see the church as an opportunity to prove that we were good human beings too. We all liked to speak for God. Quickly I discovered that it was hard for people to disagree with God, so if you said, "The Lord told me . . . " it created instant belief in what you said; you were given instant credibility. Sadly, it also created a lot of chaos.

In the meantime, for about three weeks straight, this dream about my dad kept recurring.

It was at that time we were working with a junkie day and night. One of our practices to help someone come off drugs was to zip him up in a sleeping bag and have a couple of people literally sit on him each time he went into withdrawal. We had found this to be the most satisfactory method when a person was really serious about kicking the drug habit.

We had gone three nights with this kid named Bill until he finally broke its hold. The sweating and hallucinations had stopped and it was now time for us all to get some sleep. The freed kid had finally fallen into a peaceful sleep, with the gasp, "Oh, Jesus, thank you! Thank you!" I loved seeing the demon of drugs defeated. It gave me such an exhilarated feeling of accomplishment. The Lord was really using Marge, my friends and me to help people get freed from drugs.

On the fourth night, I finally collapsed on the bed for a good night's sleep. Once again, the dream about Pop came. Only, this time, it was me in the dream as a little boy. I saw myself running away from the school playground, after having thrown the book at Mrs. Comby's stomach. I heard her cry out in anguish. Strangely enough, the voice in the dream that spoke wasn't Pop's; it was my own. Every time I opened my mouth, out would come: "Ron Rearick, you're *no* good and you're *not* going to amount to anything!"

It was horrifying to me. I woke up. It was about 3:30 in the morning, so I got up and went to the kitchen to fix myself some instant coffee. As I watched the little brown crystals disappear into the brown, syrupy blend of coffee and sugar, I was lost in a daze. I knew coffee was probably the worst thing I could drink, but I wasn't able to sleep anyway.

I sat down and tried to pray and read, but I couldn't seem to shake the little boy in my dream who kept saying, "Ron Rearick, you're *no* good. You're *never* going to amount to anything!"

I turned to the Lord, "What is it, Lord? What is it you're trying to say to me? What is it that's happening to me?"

I'd heard that the devil attacked people, so I wondered if he was trying to keep me from sleeping. But, somehow,

I knew it was deeper than that. It had to be part of my inner self being touched by the Holy Spirit. I remembered that someone had told me about this kind of phenomenon. From somewhere deep inside, I became aware of that voice again, this time saying, "Ron, you're going to have to make peace with your dad."

But how could I possibly make peace with someone who was dead? Finally, it dawned on me: I needed to forgive my dad. The meaning of the recurrent dream began to unravel, and the Lord helped me to understand as I read the Bible and talked to Him about it. I found myself, once again, having the Presence of God come upon me in an increased way that I'd come to recognize as the Holy Spirit doing a special work in me.

The Spirit helped me to realize that Pop was just a little boy who had never grown up. He was just a little boy in a big man's body. Repeatedly, I found myself speaking this amazing revelation out loud. "My dad was a little boy who never grew up." When I had finished examining this, I knew it was time to commit it to prayer.

"Lord, I forgive Pop. I forgive Smiley Rearick for being so wrong, Lord. Forgive me, Lord, for believing that I was no good and that I would never amount to anything. Thank you, God! You did have something better for me . . . and, Lord, I forgive him. I pray you would forgive him, too."

The peace flowed over me. I was now at peace with the world, and I was now at peace with myself. Somehow, I knew I had just come through one of the greatest battles of my life, and I had won!

That night I slept better than I had in months. Marge didn't even know I'd been up. I slipped back under the warm covers, said a final "Thank you, Jesus" and dropped off into a peaceful sleep.

Before I dropped off though, I glanced over at Marge sleeping peacefully, and I smiled. I thought of young Bill, who had that same night won his battle against drugs. "Life's just beginning—a new kind of life with a new kind of vision. Ron Rearick *is* good and Ron Rearick *is* amounting to something, because of Jesus!"

19

Overcoming Obstacles

After a few months in Salt Lake, word about my testimony had gotten around. I was asked to tell my incredible story at Full Gospel Businessmen meetings. The Kiwanis Club asked me to come and tell them how I'd been freed from drugs. My story came up on radio shows. I'd even been invited to speak in several neighboring cities—but I was still on parole.

Marge had never complained, but I hated not being able to leave Salt Lake without checking in with my parole officer first, or having to return on time. I was required to make biweekly visits to his office. It was the last sign of bondage from my past and I chafed at having to report and being checked up on.

As I was driving around one afternoon, I found myself saying, "Lord, you said you'd free me, but I can't even leave Salt Lake when I want to. It's like the final stage of bondage. I have to call in. I have to call out. I have to report. I have to say when I'll be there. I have to say where I'm going. I hate it. Lord, you said in your Word that I would be free . . . that whomever you set free, would be free indeed. Well, I'm *not* free!"

Like a flash, it came to me. I was supposed to tell my parole officer what had happened to me. Marge and I had been asked to come and share our testimonies in a church in a small town in western Wyoming. So I decided that when I went in to report I'd tell my parole officer what I was going to do on my out-of-town trip. We walked in the door. As usual, his secretary asked us to take a seat. We waited, and waited and waited.

It became obvious that the parole officer had far more work than he could handle. I knew it wasn't his fault that we had to wait so long. As far as I was concerned, Officer Larry was a heckuva nice guy. When Larry invited me into his office, Marge waited outside. He was always so nice to her. He appeared to be honestly thrilled that I had finally married someone who was obviously such a nice, decent person.

We sat down in his office. "Well, Ron, I understand you want to go out of town again."

"Yeah, Officer Larry, I've got something to do. I want to tell you about it."

"Okay, Ron. What do you want to tell me about?"

"Well, you know that Jesus set me free. And that's what I do. I tell people how Jesus got me out of McNeil Island Prison, how Jesus helped me to get off drugs and how Jesus gave me a beautiful wife. Larry, do you know I don't even smoke anymore?"

I didn't mean to embarrass him, but could tell I had, for he glanced down at the cigarette in his hand, then pressed it hard into the ashtray so that even the ember at the end of the cigarette was extinguished.

Larry cleared his throat. "Is that right, Ron? I'm really pleased to hear that. Go on."

I continued, "And do you know, I think the Lord wants me to tell you how I got out of prison." I began to relate to him how I'd been sentenced to 25 years by Judge Ritter.

Occasionally, he would interrupt. "Yes, Ron, I read the file."

I was warming up to my story. "In fact, do you know, Larry, that Jesus Christ got me out of prison so I could help other kids and other people kick drugs?"

As I reached into my testimony and told Larry how I'd even come to be at peace with my father, he showed increasing interest and excitement. About then, he said, "Just a minute, Ron. I want some other people to hear this too."

He buzzed the intercom and a couple of other parole officers came in. Even an FBI agent came from down the hall. "I want you guys to hear this story."

It was the second time I'd been asked to tell my story to a small group. Several were now there, waiting to hear me. It was apparent they were all interested. I led them through my whole story again, telling them how Jesus had set me free. It was an exciting afternoon for me. They were all obviously impressed and believed what I had to say.

When I finished Officer Larry said, "Fellows, I'm letting Ron go out of town this weekend. I don't know about you, but I'm really impressed with what he had to say."

They all nodded their heads in agreement and shook my hand as we walked out the door to the waiting room. I introduced each of them to Margie. I could see they thought I'd married a real beaut.

I left that office a proud man. I didn't know what would

come of it, but I knew I wanted to be completely free of having to report to my parole officer. I'd never brought up the issue before. I just hoped that I'd sown the seed that would lead to that.

Just being able to tell my story to these officers got me so enthused; the adrenalin was really pumping through me. It was truly exciting for me to tell it to people who obviously didn't believe such marvelous things could happen. They knew they were looking at and listening to a real live miracle.

Iceman was now Puddle Man.

We loaded Dina's stuffed bunnies and all our suitcases into the back of the car and headed for Wyoming, excited that I'd been able to share my faith with some real straights. We weren't sure they actually understood it all, but we did feel they got the point that Jesus was definitely someone interested in them also.

We prayed again that evening when we arrived in Wyoming. We knelt down and asked the Lord to take charge of reporting to my parole officer and thanked Him for setting me free.

* * * * * *

By now, a number of speaking opportunities were pouring in. My lack of education made me quite nervous, however, having always been intimidated by not being able to read—a fear I carried with me since grade school.

The thought of having to read the Bible aloud in public still frightened me. Before I would share my story, if I were planning to use Scripture, I'd spend two or three hours reading the biblical text over and over because I didn't want to risk anyone laughing at me.

Marge was a great teacher, though. She spent hours just reading the Bible along with me. I would read a paragraph; then she would read it through again, correcting any words I mispronounced. She also helped me with my vocabulary. Words that in the past made me tremble with fear now became easy to pronounce. Her patience and love helped me to progress at a steady pace.

I discovered that even when I did mispronounce a word, missed words, skipped over them or used the wrong word, the patience and lovingkindness of people encouraged me to go on.

My insecurities and anxieties over being wanted, liked or good enough for other people gradually disappeared. I have Margie to thank for that. She was a wonderful encourager. She always told me how well I'd spoken that evening, even when we both knew I hadn't done well at all.

* * * * * *

The trip through Wyoming was a fruitful time, though unpredictable, as those early days of public speaking were hard for me. Several received the Lord. A number of alcoholics were set free. At every place there seemed to be parents who asked us to talk to their kid, who was strung out on either psychedelics or cocaine. Even in the small towns in Utah and Wyoming, there seemed to be a mother or grandmother asking us to stop and share with their kid. We saw many changed lives. It was getting so exciting to see the impact that God was having through us in destroying the drug scene, that earlier I'd been so instrumental in promoting.

We all returned from the weekend trip enthusiastic

about the marvelous things that had occurred. As soon as I returned, I was supposed to report to Officer Larry. On Tuesday afternoon, as scheduled, I parked our used VW van in front of the building. As I left the van, I patted the front fender. It wasn't anything like the flashy number I drove when I worked for Vic Galli, but we were after a new look now. I walked into the building and grabbed a newspaper with my last quarter as I waited for the elevator. I casually watched the floor numbers flash by, got off at my floor, took a right and walked into the Probation Office.

Reporting usually took about 15 minutes. By now, I'd done it so often, I knew the procedure by rote. I walked up to the desk. "I'm here, reporting from my weekend's duty. Will you let Larry know I'm in?"

The secretary looked up. "Just a second. I'll buzz him, but I don't think he really wants to see you today, Mr. Rearick."

Now, I wasn't going to take any chances that this chick might have it wrong, so I countered, "Look, I need to check in. I've been gone for three days and I'm supposed to let him know I'm back in town."

She rang Larry. "I have Ron Rearick here in the lobby reporting from his weekend trip. Would you like to speak to him?" There was a pause. "Yes, sir, I'll tell him."

Hanging up the phone, she looked up at me. "He says you don't need to report anymore, Mr. Rearick. He says, in fact, just to notify him when you have a change of address and that will be plenty good enough for him. He'll call you once in a while to make sure things are okay, but he says he really doesn't need to see you anymore."

I turned away, then turned back. I wasn't going to risk having this secretary get things messed up, so I pursued. "Now wait a minute. You know what will happen to me if I don't show and he's mistaken or you're mistaken. They're going to lock me up again. I can't risk that. I've got to hear from him."

She looked a little annoyed as she answered, "You've got to trust me, Mr. Rearick. He meant exactly what he said. He's in conference now anyway. I will have him send you a letter confirming this."

Within five days, the letter came in the mail. It was addressed to me on official stationery. It read:

> Dear Ron:
> You are hereby released on your own recognizance, with the registering of your place of residence and place of employment. Have a great life, Son!
>
> Yours, Officer Larry

I was *free!* Hooray! I was free to do what my heart wanted me to do, free to follow Jesus anywhere, anytime!

That night, we had a great party. We went down to the Safeway Store and purchased a birthday cake to celebrate the momentous occasion! Although it was a little uncomfortable talking to Dina about being in the pen, she seemed to understand and was just as delighted as Marge and I. I was finally free from the last bondage of my terrible past, free to go wherever I felt God wanted me to go.

* * * * * *

Studying the Bible now became a consuming passion. In fact, we even found time to take several courses from Elim Bible Institute in Lima, New York. I searched out people to teach me. I couldn't learn enough.

More and more opportunities to share our testimonies at all kinds of meetings were coming our way. It was always exciting to see people respond to the Lord. A vision began to fill my heart—a vision to see kids reached and touched for God.

Now I was able to identify the reason why I was released by Judge Ritter. I now knew why I hadn't picked up the phone the day after I was released from McNeil Island Prison to order a gun, a vehicle and a supply of dope to once again set up a drug-trafficking business. On that great day, I remembered hearing myself: "If I can just keep even one kid from going the way I have, I'm going to live my life for that."

20

Finding My Niche

We eventually found ourselves in Riverton, Wyoming, where we had been invited to be pastors of a small church. We were given a free trailer to live in, and things looked great. It seemed like a big step, but the best thing for us at the time.

We loaded up the car and headed out, waving good-bye to our Salt Lake City friends with tears in our eyes. They had laid hands on us and prayed over us, believing that Jesus would help us to be His hands and heart in a small community that was hurting so badly.

There were many alcoholics in Riverton. It was a lonely little town and there wasn't a lot of excitement to take people's minds off their problems, so they drank. I'd already gained a good reputation in this community and they figured we would build a lively church that would soon be bursting at the seams.

In the early days the church did grow quickly. We were all excited and on fire. Things were really humming. Another site was located on which to build a larger church. The congregation expanded rapidly. But after several months, I discovered there was much more to being a pastor than first meets the eye. I was surprised to learn that people were saying bad things about me. I was also surprised at the mistakes I was making.

Those were painful days. We learned that not everything goes well for Christians. At that time, the book of Peter became popular with me. It spoke of suffering and being open to make adjustments. The realization came that being a Christian didn't mean everything would always be perfect.

After several months of soul-searching and anguish, we decided to figure out where the Lord would have us go and what He would have us do. We knew we weren't cut out to be pastors. We felt we were called to be evangelists, but we didn't exactly know what that entailed. We knew we enjoyed speaking in churches, but pastoring the group in Riverton made it difficult to accept all the invitations being proffered.

One day, while contemplating as a family what we should do, I told Marge I was going to take a walk down the dirt road that stretched for several miles in front of our house. As I walked, I thought about the meaning of the term *gospel*—a good story. The meaning was accurate; it was a story. But it wasn't just a story about men in general. It was the story of one particular man—the Son of God.

In my case, this was why people got excited when they heard it, because my story was not only true and so real, but it was also filled with hope: that God could release others from their prisons, whatever they might be. Not everybody had experienced penitentiary-type life, but everyone I had encountered was in some kind of prison with just as much bondage attached to it as if it were a real prison. Just hearing my story enabled so many to be released from the bondages that had captured them.

As I walked down the road, the parable about the steward came to me. As I turned that story over in my mind, I felt the Lord say: "Ron, I've entrusted you with a story of liberation. Just tell your story everywhere you go and, as you tell your story, I will begin my story in many other people."

When I returned from the walk and shared with Marge and Dina what had happened, we decided we were through with pastoring and would, instead, make ourselves available to go wherever the Lord led us. It was exciting to have speaking invitations come to us from all over the country.

My friend Ben from Salt Lake, who had taken me under his wing, had accepted a pastorate at a church in Helena, Montana, called Helena Foursquare Church. As Marge and I were burned-out after our first pastoral experience, we felt we would be safe with our friends in Helena. So we decided to locate in Helena and travel all over the United States telling our stories, using that city as our headquarters.

We soon found ourselves booked on the "Praise the Lord" (PTL) show, being met at the airport and loaded into a limousine. I remember how excited we were as we pulled up to the motel. They had our bags taken to our room and later picked us up to take us to the TV studio. I had only a quarter in my pocket and we all chuckled about it on the way. Who else but Jesus could get you a limousine ride with only a quarter to your name!

We also appeared several times on "The 700 Club," Christian Broadcasting Network, to tell our stories. The studio phones always seemed to light up when we told our experiences.

* * * * * *

One day, an invitation came to speak at a high school assembly and to talk to the students about drugs. I couldn't imagine talking to a group of kids in school. After all, school hadn't exactly been my favorite place; nevertheless, we decided to give it a try.

It was a moderately-sized high school with about 1,000 students in attendance. When I walked into the principal's office, I was quite nervous. He could tell I was, too, but he quickly put me at ease. The principal was a Christian and obviously loved his students. "Well, Ron," he said, "take a seat."

I glanced up at the American flag that hung in the corner of his office. It brought back memories of my own school days. In fact, it reminded me of my last day in school in the eighth grade, when I stood under the same kind of flag, announcing to the school officials I was quitting.

A little self-consciously I grinned and said, "It's good to be here, Sir."

The principal then prepared me for the assembly. "You've got to be careful about talking about the Lord you know, the separation of Church and State thing. But, Ron, do enough to be helpful to us today."

When I walked into the assembly the gym was packed full. As I was about to be introduced, I overheard the vice principal talking to the principal. "Are you sure he can handle this crowd? You know they've shaken up the last three speakers pretty badly. We don't want them to know this is a drug conversation either."

The principal glanced over at me. "Ron, do you think you can handle these kids? They've eaten up the best so far."

I shot a glance around the large, noise-filled hall. "Well, we'll see, won't we?"

Under my breath I prayed. "Oh, Lord Jesus, I really don't know how to talk to these kids. I don't know how you got me into this, but, Lord, please help me. Let your Presence that filled that cell, Lord, now fill this room."

As we walked to the speaker's platform, I kept muttering and praying. The principal called the assembly to order, and introduced me.

"Students, this is Ron Rearick, Iceman, who has a fascinating story to tell. Some of you have already heard him in your classes and, evidently, you really enjoyed his story, so he's here now to tell it to all of you."

I stepped to the microphone and effortlessly began to speak. Even I was surprised. The nervousness and apprehension were gone. I shared with them about the serious drug problem in America and my previous involvement in it and other illegal activities. I could see excitement shining in their eyes when I told about going to South America, and bringing back cocaine. I also told about some of the narrow escapes I'd had. Their attention was riveted on me as I took them through one sordid episode after another in my life. I told them what the Mafia stood for and how every time the kids bought a joint they were paying for some guy to abuse kids. When they did that, they were like stockholders supporting a company in an illegal industry that enslaved people to drug addiction. It was gratifying to see their enlightenment.

Then I shared with the assembly how a totally depraved man like me could be completely freed from the bondages of my past: I was a man who figured he would never be any good nor amount to anything. I was a man who had committed every imaginable crime short of mur-

187

der. I had committed terrible atrocities on others. Then a fellow inmate handed me a Bible and told me of a better way. I simply got down on my knees one night in my jail cell and asked God to forgive me and free me. In a matter of time, God turned my life full circle.

With tears in my eyes, I looked intently into the upturned faces of all those youngsters and finished. "Kids, there's a better way for you too, a much better way."

When I concluded, I looked over at the principal, fully expecting that the kids would jump up and scurry from the auditorium. Instead, all was silent. Then, in one accord, the entire assembly stood to their feet, clapping and cheering. It was almost as though they were cheering for themselves. If they had only known what that meant to me. That day was the start of God's fulfilling a dream He had placed in my heart.

One after another, following their dismissal, students came up and grabbed my hand. "Ron, thank you!" and "Ron, that was phenomenal!" Five or six teachers thanked me.

Students lined up to have me talk and pray with them individually. During the question-and-answer time, there were 30 or 40 kids standing around me. One asked, "Are you a Christian? You mentioned you were handed a Bible."

Then I was able to share fully what it meant to be born again. Several received the Lord that day as their Saviour.

On the way out, the principal put his arm around my shoulder. "Ron, you did a phenomenal job today. I don't know how you did it, but you can come back anytime you want."

Again, tears glistened in my eyes. "If I can keep even one kid in school to get an education and keep him away from drugs, that's what I live for now."

In the months following our first school assembly, word spread quickly throughout the Northwest and elsewhere, which gained us entrance into many schools. I now realized clearly that my main purpose in life would be to share the "good story" of Jesus as it applied to my life with as many students as possible in schools across America.

Even the Pentagon invited me to Washington to do a series of video tapes against drug abuse. In addition, I became the proud possessor of a plaque from Mrs. Nancy Reagan, expressing her appreciation for my volunteer efforts to help curb the drug culture in the United States.

I remember how excited we were when the plaque arrived. I couldn't believe it. Can you imagine that—me, Ron Rearick from Salt Lake City, Utah, Iceman, receiving a commendation from the wife of the President of the United States of America?!

The day arrived when we were to leave Helena and move to Kirkland, Washington. It was tough to leave, as we were particularly concerned about the strong drug culture in that area. But we were also concerned about drug problems on the West Coast and felt drawn to the congregation of Eastside Foursquare Church in a suburb of Greater Seattle. Eastside became our home and, eventually, we became staff pastors and evangelists, supporting the pastoral ministry there. It has allowed us to travel all around the country, yet still have a home to return to.

It is good to be home. We knew when we moved into this community that we would be here a long time. The restlessness has totally left my life.

A strong feeling has been birthed in my heart. I have become more and more convinced that one man can do much to help curb the demon influence of drugs in our society. Hatred for the thing that I had once been so much a part of has now filled my life. Compassion, not condemnation, characterizes my response to others who have been trapped by drug addiction. After all, how could a man like me criticize anyone else? Drug addicts, prostitutes, the lonely, the rich and successful, the poor can all experience what I have received from God.

* * * * * *

On one of my trips to speak in schools and prisons, I landed in Harrisburg, Pennsylvania. Before this particular trip had commenced, I had received notice that I was to receive an honor as the first passenger on American Airlines' inaugural flight from Harrisburg to Chicago.

When my secretary handed the notice to me, I chuckled, believing it was a joke. After all, everyone in the office knew I'd extorted a million dollars from United Airlines in 1972, and there were always little jabs and jokes about having our own financial wizard on staff. So I was curious as to what kind of honor it could be.

Having spoken at several penitentiaries and schools around Harrisburg, it was now time to board Flight No 673 on July 2, 1984. I remember how surprised we were when we pulled up to the airport and saw so many dignitaries collected under the large yellow canopy on the taxiway. We joked together that they must have received word that I was coming.

There were hors d'oeuvres everywhere and it looked like a very impressive promotional affair. The young woman, who had evidently sent me the letter, was prepared to meet me as I came through the ticket line. The ticket taker at the airlines desk nodded to her. "This is Mr. Rearick, Susan. He's your guest of honor today."

I walked out on the taxi apron carrying the little blue book about my life story. As Susan handed me the first-class ticket to Chicago and a plaque, I handed her the book.

I expected that she would read it later on, but she flipped it over and started reading right then about Iceman, the man who extorted a million dollars from United Airlines and was sentenced to 25 years at McNeil Island Federal Penitentiary.

She blanched and walked over to the group of airlines officials. They huddled in a circle, talking excitedly. Since 1972, I'd become a little edgy about flying. When I did, I remained serious and was careful of every word I spoke, lest I be misunderstood and end up in an interrogation room if they found out who I was. I figured it would take months to straighten out a misunderstanding like that.

I thought I'd better explain to them that I wasn't that way anymore and that I wasn't trying to steal a million dollars. I approached the circle of agitated people. "Hey, that's not me anymore. I'm not . . . " I began to stutter.

The American Airlines president glanced up from the circle, took the young woman's arm who was in charge of the presentation and hurried over. "Son, we're going to make a big splash today."

With that, the news cameras zoomed in, we boarded the plane and all settled down for the flight to Chicago. I was able to share a seat with the president himself. We had a wonderful snack en route. I was also given the opportunity to tell him my life story and how the Lord had changed it so dramatically. He was obviously impressed.

Once again, I was moved by the humor and direction the Lord had taken in my life. After all, who but the Lord would set up such an elaborate scheme to have Iceman, the extortioner of a million dollars from one airline, be the honored passenger of another airline just 12 years later! I couldn't wait to share with my family, pastor and friends what had happened on the runway at Harrisburg.

* * * * * *

As part of the continuing saga of God's grace in my life, I thought back to an assembly at a mixed-race school where about half of the students were White, a quarter Orientals and a quarter Hispanics. It was a great experience for me, and it was exciting to see how my message of Jesus could bring unity in a situation that appeared to be so absent of His Presence.

As we pulled into the parking lot that day, we could smell the sickly sweet scent of marijuana wafting over the parking lot. It was difficult to determine which circle of youngsters was smoking—perhaps they all were.

When I walked down the hall with the two fellows who had come with me, I noticed that holes had been poked in the ceiling with what looked like cue sticks. We were advised to be careful about going into the restrooms alone. Most of the restroom doors had been torn off the stalls and they were dangerous places for the uninitiated in the art of warfare.

Despite initial appearances, the Iceman story went over big. Once again, following the assembly's conclusion, the students gave me a standing ovation. On this occasion, I had been offered a counseling room for several hours so I could talk to students with problems.

I was introduced to a young man named Davey. He had threatened to kill some of the Hispanics who he believed had participated in his brother's murder. The thought of revenge consumed him. You could see it in his eyes. I'd seen this same look in my own eyes many times when I looked in the mirror. It was the look of defiance and violent retaliation.

Now several weeks later he was in my office waiting for my return from Pennsylvania. I opened the conversation. "Hey, Davey, what's happenin', Man?"

Coldly, he stared back at me. "Hey, the shrink said I ought to talk to you. That's the only reason I'm here, Man. It's really quite a story, but you can't help me, Man. I'm under control."

I began to share with him how my old man had always said I'd never amount to anything, that I was no good and how dangerous I became when I believed that. I talked to him about forgiveness. Then I reached out and took his arm. I saw traces of drug use on his arm, and his eyes had that look that I'd come to know so well—the look that would lead him down a dead-end path, probably even wind up murdered some day on the street.

"Davey, I believe in you. I also believe that God's got something better for you. Davey, did you know you can be just about anything you want to be in life? You can be a tough guy. You can be a druggie. In fact, you can even be a fagot. But, Davey, the war inside you can now be over, if you want it to be."

I explained to him about the wonderful peace that had come to me when I was finally able to face my own feelings about my dad. It seems that Davey's family had blamed him for what happened to his brother. It had a ring of familiarity as I remembered my own turmoil over the loss of my own brother Donny. I could see that the problem here was Davey's blaming himself for his brother's murder—just as I had thought I was to blame for my brother's death.

193

Davey had become a ring leader around school in drugs and violence.

Seeing the similarity in our lives about our brothers gave me the opportunity to tell him how I always felt that I was not as smart or as good as my brother, and that if Donny had only lived longer, the whole world would have been a better place. That I felt I was a poor substitute for Donny.

Davey's eyes lit up. I could see the melting process starting—the same warming that happened in my heart 12 years earlier. I encouraged him not to take revenge over his brother's death, because Jesus had already taken the punishment for everybody. What Jesus had done was exciting, for it allowed me to be able to forgive my dad, even though I'd been taken advantage of, because there was no more punishment to be given. Jesus had taken the punishment for all of us when He died on the cross so many years ago on Calvary.

"Man, all you've got to do is just forgive your folks and say, 'Thank you, Jesus, that you took care of this in my heart.'"

Davey asked, "Hey, Man, will you pray with me? I want to know what you know."

We reached across the table to each other. Once again I was filled with excitement at seeing someone being freed from the lies that bound him. We began to pray. I began; he repeated:

"Lord Jesus . . . Lord Jesus; I forgive . . . I forgive; And, Lord, I give you my whole life now . . . And, Lord, I give you my whole life now."

"Lord, melt me as you did Iceman," Davey added.

What exciting words to hear! Another triumph through the love of Jesus!

Marge had met me at SeaTac International Airport that morning on my return from Harrisburg with an urgent appeal to meet with Davey and to talk him out of committing suicide. He had been waiting for my return before going through with it. Once again I realized that the only tool I had was a story—the good story of Jesus!

By the time we had finished praying, I was prepared to plop down in my chair, put my feet up on my desk counter and continue telling Marge about what had happened the past few days: how successful we had been in the prisons and how terrific the kids had been in the assemblies. Something caught my eye. A great big sign had been placed on my desk: "Welcome Home, Puddle Man!" I grinned widely. The meltdown was continuing on schedule.

Epilogue

I'm sure you found the story of Iceman exciting. It was very thrilling for me to be part of retelling Ron's story.

If you are interested, as many people are, in getting more materials from Iceman, or if you would like to purchase the videotape of his testimony, or schedule Ron to speak at school assemblies or to your congregation, please write:

Ron Rearick
c/o Born to Choose
P.O. Box 536
Kirkland, WA 98083-0536

or call us at 206/823-2033.

A parting word: I encourage you to share with others the story of Iceman, as well as your own story of the life of Jesus in you.

If you would like to receive Jesus or to know more about what it is like to be a Christian, please feel free to contact us. We will be happy to direct you to someone who will be happy to share a meaningful understanding of what Christ can do in your life.

Sincerely,

Pastor Doug Murren